A STRUCTURAL THEORY
OF THE EMOTIONS

A STRUCTURAL THEORY OF THE EMOTIONS

JOSEPH DE RIVERA

With an Introductory Essay by

HARTVIG DAHL

Psychological Issues
Monograph 40

INTERNATIONAL UNIVERSITIES PRESS, INC.
New York

Library of Congress Cataloging in Publication Data

De Rivera, Joseph.
    A structural theory of the emotions.
        (Psychological issues ; v. 10, no. 4 : Monograph ; 40)
    Bibliography: p.
    Includes index.
    1. Emotions. I. Title. II. Series.
[DNLM: 1. Emotions. 2. Interpersonal relations.
W1 PS572 v.10 no. 4 / BF531 D433s]
BF531.D38   152.4   76-53916
ISBN 0-8236-6171-7
ISBN 0-8236-6170-9 pbk.

Manufactured in the United States of America

CONTENTS

CONSIDERATIONS FOR A THEORY OF EMOTIONS

Hartvig Dahl

There are few indisputable facts about emotions and there is no single widely accepted theory about emotions. The plethora of theories, large and small, complex and limited, similar and contradictory, compellingly reminds us (as it has de Rivera) of the fable of the blind men separately examining and describing the elephant. It is a tempting metaphor for the state of confusion in the field of emotions. But it is a misleading one because its images gently reinforce our wish to believe that there is indeed an elephant standing around waiting to be seen if only we open our eyes. The metaphor also deceives in a subtler way, for by naming the elephant we unwittingly encourage our own conviction that we will recognize the animal if we see it. We may never have encountered a snark, but who has not seen an elephant? So what is the moral to the story (for all fables must have morals)? The moral is that our task is not to find the elephant and take a good look at it. Rather our task is to understand that we have to create the beast. We have to construct it from fragmented parts, fiddle with it here and there, and change it from time to time as we find necessary. And if we name it an elephant we must keep in mind that when we create new models we may in fact be creating new species with unexpected properties.

And so it is with emotions. If we begin by asking what an emotion *is* we soon find that we are instead asking a whole set of other questions, such as: What does an emotion feel like? Where do we feel it? How do we express it? What apparatus produces it? On and on. The early history of theories of emotions is by and large the history of attempts to answer single questions. In the language of the fable we have looked at a leg here and a trunk there as well as a tusk, a tail, and a hide. Plutchik (1962) understood this and sensibly entitled his first chapter, "What is a Theory of Emotion?" rather than, What is an Emotion? After asking 18 questions he asserted that "any adequate theory should either provide an answer (even if tentative) to each of these questions, or indicate the kind of evidence that must be sought in order to answer them" (p. 6). The choices of what question to ask, as we ought to expect, have historically been determined by such incidental considerations as: a larger interest (Darwin [1872]—variation and inheritance of behavior), easily accessible data (James [1890]—introspection), the hysterical symptoms of Viennese women (Freud—psychoanalysis), a theoretical commitment (Miller [1951]—intervening variables in learning experiments), or a preoccupation with how the brain works (Cannon [1927]—neurophysiology).

And then the answers to the questions begin to influence the shape of our conception of what an emotion *is*. The theoretical constructs and their illustrations (or embodiments) in models begin to take on a life of their own and represent themselves as the whole creature. Thus James (1890) could assert that "bodily changes follow directly the perception of the exciting fact, and ... our feeling of the same changes as they occur IS the emotion" (p. 449). The error in such an assertion that is of interest here lies in the implication that an emotion *is* bodily changes. And although this particular misconception is by now well understood, there are many other examples of components passing themselves off as whole creatures. Clearly the ideal correction of this kind of error is to construct theories (and models) which integrate the component constructions.

Plutchik, for example, has elaborated a structural model based on an analogy with some characteristics of light. He postulates eight pure emotions which mix with each other according to certain specified principles, much the way we think of pure colors in the light spectrum mixing to form the large variety of discriminable colors. My point here is not to characterize his theory adequately but to ask how we could evaluate its fitness as a candidate for the whole creature called Emotion. He suggests four criteria (and others could be added): (1) A theory's integrative power, i.e., the comprehensiveness of the "facts" that it can in some sense explain; (2) its power to stimulate research, i.e., its capacity to reveal what we do not know; (3) its predictive power, i.e., its ability to suggest new relationships or how to find such relationships; and (4) its generality, i.e., its fruitfulness in suggesting connections with seemingly unrelated constructs and "facts" from other areas of inquiry.

We are all at least implicitly aware of the usual scientific procedures by which we evaluate a theory on such criteria as these. But when we have done all the experiments which can be done, when we have checked all the "facts," when we have thoroughly examined the logic, there usually remains a residue of judgment which can only be called esthetic. Such judgments are complex, often tacit, discriminations, more often felt than thought. Issues of subtlety, of elegance of constructs and relationships, of satisfying but not jarring simplicity, and of apt choice of metaphors are often decisive factors in our acceptance of the "reality" implied by a theory.

I put the word "reality" in quotation marks in order to imply both real and not real simultaneously. I mean it in the sense that the mere existence of a construct (and its surrounding theory), for example, an *electron, unconscious fantasy,* or *deep structure,* gives the theoretical construct a certain status as a thing, a quality of thingness, of existence. And what we know about the thingness is defined by the theory itself. Nagel (1961) wrote, "What it is to be a molecule, for example, is prescribed by the assumptions of the theory. Indeed, there is no way of ascertaining what is the 'nature' of molecules except by examining the postulates of the molecular theory" (p. 92).

In the sense that the physical world of atomic and subatomic particles (or waves) is truly a constructed world, and in the sense that the personal historical psychological world of a psychoanalytic patient is a constructed world, the world of *emotion* will be constructed by an adequate theory of emotions. Only as we reach a consensus on a comprehensive theory can we in any accurate sense say we know what we mean when we answer the question, What *is* an *emotion?*

We should not be at all surprised if this truism (for so I regard it) is ignored in practice, because each theoretician inevitably develops a strong narcissistic investment in his own significant creations. Lay persons may imagine that scientists are a cool, dispassionate lot, ready to abandon their theories at the first drop of contrary "facts." But scientists labor under no such illusions—except perhaps as applied to others than themselves! Although the investigator may remain deliberately detached in everyday, routine work, once he has constructed a full-blown theory he is typically thoroughly committed to it and will defend it with all the dogged resourcefulness of a loving mother protecting her young child. This is why we need the elaborate procedures of the scientific method—to help us select the most promising theoretical offspring independently of the adoration bestowed upon them by their admiring creators.

Thus far I have asserted that a comprehensive theory of emotions remains only a goal. I have also meant to imply that we probably have some distance to go before we reach that goal. In the meantime we are left with a large number of hypotheses, partial theories, models, and even a new action language (Schafer, 1976) for emotions. Given the disparate assortment of ideas available, our problem is to select those worthy of serious pursuit. I regard de Rivera's (1962, 1977) theories of emotions as particularly interesting contenders for our attention.

What originally attracted me to de Rivera's (1962) doctoral dissertation and its elegant "geometry" of emotions was my own esthetic preference for abstract dimensional models (see also Wundt, 1907; Freud, 1915; Tolman, 1923; Schlosberg, 1954; Osgood, Suci, and Tannenbaum, 1957; Davitz, 1969). It was a theory which integrated the major psychological theories and models up to that time. De Rivera's "decision theory" postulated that a person experiences a particular emotion (an "end decision") as a result of separate decisions on six abstractly defined independent dimensions. Five of these dimensions consisted of two states (binary) and one of three states (ternary). Independent decisions on each of these dimensions yielded 96 $[3 \cdot 2^5]$ intersections, each uniquely defining a single emotion.

I was so fascinated with the theory that, with the help of Barry Stengel, I did a partial replication (using only three dimensions) of de Rivera's classification of emotion words (Dahl and Stengel, in preparation). The results, while differing in certain details from de Rivera's own data, strongly confirmed his finding that people could reliably assign a large number of emotion words to one or the other polar choice on each dimension. Later I adapted and integrated three of de Rivera's dimensions into a new psychoanalytic model of motivation (Dahl, in press).

Meanwhile, de Rivera's interest in phenomenology blossomed. And this vastly different conceptual framework led him to question the adequacy of sequential, mechanistic theoretical models such as the decision theory. Instead, he began to focus on the interrelationships among emotions, and he created new constructs that would help to explicate those relationships. The dimensions, which had been no more than a classification scheme in the first theory, were transformed into a system designed to specify how each different emotion is related to every other emotion. In so doing he defines a structure of emotional relationships that fundamentally govern object relationships. This structure is the subject matter of the new theory (de Rivera, 1977).

From a psychoanalyst's point of view, a major strength of both theories lies in the choice of a subject-object polarity as one of the abstract dimensions. Quite independently of Freud (1915), de Rivera understood that there was more to the subject-object distinction than the mere difference between emotions with and those without external objects. Most emotion theorists make such a discrimination between what de Rivera calls the "it" emotions (those that have an object) and the "me" emotions (those in which the self is the implicit object). But de Rivera goes beyond this to propose that the me emotions are specific transformations of it emotions.

It is implicit in his theories that these transformations may occur under three main conditions: (1) When one is the recipient of someone else's it emotion directed toward oneself; (2) when one projects onto someone else an it emotion and then perceives that emotion as directed toward onself; and (3) when one internalizes an object to whom one ascribes (either realistically or by projection) an it emotion directed toward oneself. Thus, if one perceives that another person holds him in *contempt* (an it emotion) he is likely to feel *shame* (a me emotion), and if one internalizes (as in identification with) a person who holds him in contempt he is likely to have an enduring disposition to feel shame. In similar fashion *love* transforms to *security, fear* to *anxiety, admiration* to *pride, anger* to *depression*, etc.

My concern here is not whether any specific transformation is "correct" but rather with the general principle of the transformation. The power of the concept lies in its generality — in the proposition that one can always expect to find a specific me emotion counterpart to an it emotion. Of course, psychoanalysts have often noted a few such relationships, but there is nothing in their theories which leads them to expect specifiable patterns of such transformations. On the contrary, both Brenner (1974) and Schafer (1976) hold quite the opposite view — that is, that each emotional experience is unique unto itself and specific only to the person and his situation. Those who take such positions are unlikely to find much appeal in de Rivera's new theory.

In my opinion de Rivera's theory is meant for those who seek generality, who are open to truly novel concepts, who are not put off by ambiguity, and who are willing to accept metaphorical definitions as first approximations. He focuses systematically on questions of a kind that the clinician addresses only incidentally: What are the necessary and sufficient conditions for the occurrence of a particular emotion? What is the interpersonal function of a particular emotion? What does it do to the relationship between the person and the object? In other words, what does its communication accomplish?

The theory is also meant for those who can set aside for the moment their historical perspectives and accept as valid the quite unfamiliar ahistorical—that is, cross-sectional in time—method of analysis. This is necessary in order to understand how a theory of emotions can pay so little attention to the role of pleasure and unpleasure, qualities which are prominently considered in many other theories about emotions. De Rivera does not deny that people find experiences pleasurable or unpleasurable, nor that such experience plays a role in motivating behavior. He simply takes the position that the concepts which he offers are themselves sufficient to characterize emotions. And it is emotions, not all of behavior, that his theory purports to explain. Thus pleasure, unpleasure, and pain all are involved in motivating *ongoing* behavior, but are, in his judgment, not necessary determinants of particular emotions. I think he was able to arrive at this view precisely because he takes an ahistorical position.

Nonetheless, de Rivera is quite aware that he has not succeeded in the larger task of specifying "the exact conditions under which emotion will occur" (p. 122). Here I think he offers a challenge to clinicians who take the trouble to become familar with his theory. He understands that, in order to specify the exact conditions, it will be necessary "to add a dynamic dimension to structural inquiry; ... to study concrete occurrences of emotion in the context of an individual's life" (p. 123). I take his use of the word "dynamic" to mean historical and motivational—in other words, to require the very perspective that a psychodynamically oriented clinician could bring to the investigation.

Such a reader may well find the going rough because the terms and concepts are not those with which he is familiar. Moreover, some of these terms (*movement*, for instance) are metaphorical concepts with several different, albeit related, meanings. But these are difficulties that are not unique to this theory. They are an indication of the stage of its development, for, like all theories, it is as much a process of becoming as an end result. Its present articulation is just a necessary convenience and must not be confused with the larger enterprise of continuing investigation, refinement, and creation. Of course, we are not yet ready to name it an elephant! But it is a lusty and provocative creature.

REFERENCES

Brenner, C. (1974), On the Nature and Development of Affects: A Unified Theory. *Psychoanal. Quart.*, 43:532-556.

Cannon, W. B. (1927), The James-Lange Theory of Emotions: A Critical Examination and an Alternative Theory. *Amer. J. Psychol.*, 39:106-124.

Dahl, H. (in press), The Appetite Hypothesis of Emotions: A New Psychoanalytic Model of Motivation. In: *Emotions and Psychopathology*, ed. C. E. Izard. New York: Plenum.

Dahl, H., & Stengel, B. (in preparation), A Classification of Emotion Words: A Modification and Partial Test of de Rivera's Decision Theory of Emotions.

Darwin, C. (1872), *The Expression of the Emotions in Man and Animals.* London: Murray.

Davitz, J. R. (1969), *The Language of Emotion.* New York: Academic Press.

de Rivera, J. (1962), A Decision Theory of Emotions. Doctoral dissertation, Stanford University, 1961. *Dissertation Abstracts International* (University Microfilm No. 62-2356).

———— (1977), A Structural Theory of the Emotions. *Psychol. Issues,* Monogr. No. 40. New York: International Universities Press.

Freud, S. (1915), Instincts and Their Vicissitudes. *Standard Edition,* 14:117-140. London: Hogarth Press, 1957.

James. W. (1890), *The Principles of Psychology,* Vol. 2. New York: Dover, 1950.

Miller, N. E. (1951), Learnable Drives and Rewards. In: *Handbook of Experimental Psychology*, ed. S. S. Stevens. New York: Wiley.

Nagel, E. (1961), *The Structure of Science: Problems in the Logic of Scientific Explanation.* New York: Harcourt, Brace & World.

Osgood, C. E., Suci, G. J., & Tannenbaum, P. H. (1957), *The Measurement of Meaning.* Urbana: University of Illinois Press.

Plutchik, R. (1962), *The Emotions: Facts, Theories, and a New Model.* New York: Random House.

Schafer, R. (1976), *A New Language for Psychoanalysis.* New Haven: Yale University Press.

Schlosberg, H. (1954), Three Dimensions of Emotion. *Psychol. Rev.*, 61:81-88.

Tolman, E. C. (1923), A Behavioristic Account of the Emotions. *Psychol. Rev.,* 30:217-227.

Wundt, W. (1907), *Outlines of Psychology,* trans. C. H. Judd. New York: Strechert.

PREFACE

In 1959 I began a series of interviews on the emotion of anger. These interviews were guided by the presupposition that there was an essence to the experience of anger. I believed that there must be some universal structure to the experience of anger, some common element in all cases of anger that made the experience an "anger" experience rather than an experience of love, or fear, or a stomach ache. My initial supposition was that anger always involved a desire to hurt the object of anger. However, it became apparent that this could not be maintained in all cases. The only common element seemed to be a wish to remove the cause of the anger. This more abstract wish could easily be contrasted with the wish accompanying fear—to remove the self. Then, a whole network of relations began to appear, a network that linked the different emotions to one another. In 1961 I described aspects of this structure in my doctoral thesis—*A Decision Theory of the Emotions*—and showed how the structure could account for the usage of emotion names.

In the ensuing years I have continually attempted to arrive at a more precise understanding of our emotions. I have introspected, interviewed, and read accounts of emotions until many of them have become friends and most are at least acquaintances. Nevertheless, I have yet to reach a complete understanding of the emotions, and would not have written this monograph were it not for the encouragement of Hartvig Dahl. I thought that since he had found some of the ideas stimulating for his own work, perhaps others might be interested, even though the ideas are still somewhat imprecise and unfinished. Also, I would like to share what I am doing so that others who are friends with some of the emotions might begin a correspondence.

I have already had the opportunity of enjoying the ideas of some of my colleagues. I especially want to mention the work of Fritz Heider, whose search for a structure underlying interpersonal relations lends support to my own venture; Tamara Dembo, who encouraged me to see emotions in interpersonal terms; and Isidor Chein, whose friendship and continual assertion of man-as-actor forced me to modulate my understanding of the role that emotions play in our lives. And I have greatly benefitted from innumerable dialogues with responsive and assertive students, with Joel Funk, John Lau, Jan Lindsay, and other members of the "phenomenology lunch group" at Clark University.

As a result of encounters with emotions, colleagues, and students, my understanding of the emotions has developed beyond the ideas of the original dissertation—ideas that are primarily expressed in the second chapter of this monograph. Some of the more recent work on emotions is contained in the third and fourth chapters. This work was aided by a faculty research grant from the Social Science Research Council, and I would like to take this opportunity to express my gratitude for their fellowship program—one of the few available that supports theoretical as well as empirical work. Finally, I want to thank Becky Clark for her typing, Susan Heinemann for her editing, Eric de Rivera for his draftsmanship, and my family and friends for the opportunity to experience so many emotions.

Joseph de Rivera

Chapter One

THE PHENOMENON
OF EMOTION

Emotion may be viewed in many different ways and perhaps no other subject in psychology provokes such diverse theories and attitudes. Some writers focus on the disruptive character of emotion, others on its functional significance. Some see emotions as individual entities (anger, love, joy, etc.), others insist there are no such things as emo*tions*, but only the emotion*al* (either as disrupting or as activating behavior). For some emotional experience is merely a composite of general bodily sensations, while for others emotions are the basic forces guiding life.

The word emotion derives from the Latin verb *emovere*. The term, which literally means "to move out," was initially used in the sense of moving a crowd out of the forum, soldiers out of a private home, or dirt out of an excacation; that is, in the sense of an authoritative force moving a resisting mass.[1]

Thus, the word itself captures an important feature of emotion—that we experience ourselves or the other as *being moved*. This passivity may be contrasted with our experience of willing an action, where we take responsibility for initiating a project of action leading to events that would not otherwise occur.[2] On the other hand, the experience of being moved by an emotion may be contrasted with the feeling of *having* to do something because of some external force. That is, we do not

[1] Both Pribram (Pribram and Melges, 1968) and Bowlby (1969) incorrectly translate this as "out of" or "away from" motion and suggest that the term implies a lack of movement. In fact, it implies being moved. There is a lack of *action* but not of movement.

[2] This concise analysis is stated and developed by Ricoeur (1966).

11

find ourselves acting out of habit, or because of the requirements of our situation (what is demanded by our job, by some authority, or by our ideals), or out of the force of some compulsion stemming from either the id or superego. When we are moved by emotion we feel the desire to hit, hug, or whatever, even though our judgment may check this action. This is the paradox of emotional experience—we are passively being moved rather than acting and yet this movement seems to be coming from *within* us.

In this introductory chapter I shall review the ways in which the various theories of the emotions deal with this paradox. This is more than an intellectual exercise. Each of the major theories focuses on important emotional phenomena and, thus, alerts us to the different aspects of emotion. However, I should warn the reader that the portrait of emotion that emerges from the accurate but limited accounts of these different theories resembles the picture of the proverbial elephant in darkness whose individual parts were each reasonably described by different persons.

Because it makes no sense either to refute or merely to add together the available theories, at the close of this chapter I shall sketch a radically different picture of the emotions. While my sketch responds to the different aspects of emotion revealed by previous theories, it is primarily based on an analysis of the *movement* of emotion. When we examine individual emotions they reveal different types of movement and these different types suggest that an emotion is not an isolated entity, but rather part of a *system* that governs object relations—a structure, which can only be explained if we use the dyad (instead of the individual) as the unit of analysis. First, however, let us examine the current theories of emotion.

CURRENT THEORIES OF EMOTIONS

Perhaps a hundred theories about the emotions examine the phenomena from every conceivable point of view and in the context of dozens of broader theoretical perspectives. For our purposes it will be sufficient to consider some of the major theories, together with their contemporary developments. While these theories have various points of similarity and difference, I shall classify them according to how they handle the central feature of emotion—our experience of emotion as passively moving us at the same time that it is a part of us.

The various theories of the emotions offer at least three quite different solutions to this paradox. The majority suggest that emotions are related to instincts (or some similar hypothetical construct). This idea is appealing because "instincts" provide an impulsive force that passively moves us and yet are part of our own bodies (or our unconscious self). A second class of theories relate emotion to the perception of value in the person's environment. This solution plays on the fact that values have the property of being both objective (we experience the value as belonging to the object that moves us) and subjective (the value is our own). Finally, some theories suggest that emotions are transformations of the relation between the person and his environment. In these theories, the person is conceived to be inseparable from the world in which he finds himself. The passive movement of emotion corresponds to a change in how the person exists in his world.

EMOTIONS AS RELATED TO INSTINCTS

McDougall's Theory and Direct Motivation

The essential aspects of this position are that emotions reflect a number of discrete biological entities that have arisen in the course of evolution to aid the organism in directing its behavior to deal with the environment. McDougall (1908) postulates the existence of entities which he at first calls "instincts." He states: "We may, then, define an instinct as an inherited or innate psychophysical disposition which determines the possessor to perceive, and to pay attention to, objects of a certain class, to experience an emotional excitement of a particular quality upon perceiving such an object, and to act in regard to it in a particular manner, or, at least, to experience an impulse to such action" (p. 29).

McDougall sees these instincts as being composed of an afferent, a central, and a motor part. The central part distributes the nervous impulses to the skeleton and viscera so as to execute the action effectively; the nervous activities of this central part are the correlates of emotion. The afferent and motor aspects of an instinct are open to learning and to what we now call imprinting. Modifications occur with the influence of pleasure and pain. However, the central part "retains its specific character and remains common to all individuals and all situations in which the instinct is excited" (p. 39).

McDougall believes that each instinct has an emotion whose quality is specific and peculiar to it. He lists about 14 instinct-emotions which he defines as primary because of their occurrence in the higher animals and their liability to morbidity when excessive. I have schematized his theory in Figure 1.

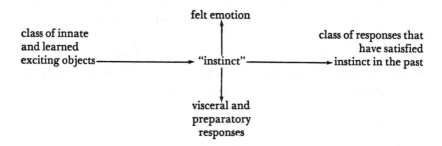

FIGURE 1. McDougall's Theory

Any object that becomes attached to an instinct can call it into play. Once aroused, the instinct mobilizes energy, causes adaptive visceral responses, and calls forth behavior that has satisfied the instinct in the past. Since emotion is the conscious representation of the instinct's central part, it is cast in a functional role and reflects the action of instinctual patterns that organize behavior.

It is perhaps unfortunate that McDougall's theory is couched in terms of instincts. He is not speaking of the stereotyped response patterns, triggered by a specific stimulus configuration, that modern ethologists term "instinctive behavior." Rather he refers to much more flexible patterns of behavior using a hypothetical construct of the type that today we might call a central instruction or a program for behavior. In fact, as is shown in Appendix A, McDougall's "instincts" are formally identical to S-R theory's "intervening responses," to Cannon's (1927) "thalamic neurons," and to many of the various central nervous system "circuits" postulated by physiological psychologists to account for emotions. Perhaps the closest contemporary theory is that of Plutchik (1962). Instead of instincts, Plutchik speaks of primary emotions—hypothetical constructs—which serve specified biological adaptive processes that relate the animal to its environment (e.g., anger and the removal of barriers to satisfaction).

The key concepts in McDougall's theory are that there are different emotional entities, each of which establishes a particular goal for behavior, and that the emotion persists until this goal is reached. For example, when we are afraid we want to escape danger, when we are angry we want to remove an obstacle, when we love we want to be close to our lover. In other words, McDougall's theory (and others in this class) emphasizes the intentional, directed aspect of emotion, an aspect often reflected in the imagery and behavior of the person experiencing the emotion. Thus, the person who is angry may wish to smack or tear apart the object of his anger, the person who loves may imagine holding his lover.

Tomkins's Theory and Secondary Motivation

Although closely related to McDougall's theory, Tomkins's (1962) theory differs in several interesting respects. First, Tomkins makes a sharp distinction between a drive system (where pleasure and pain signals involve bodily needs such as hunger and thirst) and an affect system that acts to amplify (or inhibit) drive signals and is capable of being activated independently by numerous stimuli. Like McDougall's instincts this affect system has developed in the course of evolution and is the "primary provider of blueprints for cognition, decision and action" (Tomkins, 1962, p. 22). It is of central motivational importance because its flexibility allows it to become attached to many different stimuli and responses. However, and this is the most important difference, whereas McDougall's instincts *directly* motivate instrumental behavior (e.g., fear causes one to run or to perform some other escape behavior, love causes a range of responses that protect the other), Tomkins's affect system *indirectly* motivates behavior through a variety of positive and negative signals that are inherently acceptable or unacceptable. One learns the behavior that produces acceptable rather than unacceptable signals. Whereas McDougall's system is constructed to be *hormic* or purposive, Tomkins's system is really a *hedonic* system where the organism's behavior is simply directed to get the rewards and avoid the punishments provided by emotions. In McDougall's system a person who is afraid attempts to escape and feels pleasure if he succeeds. In Tomkins's system fear emits unacceptable signals and the person performs whatever behavior will eliminate these painful signals. There are some behaviors invoked directly by Tomkins's affect system, but these are expressive rather than operationally directed and mainly involve the facial muscles. Tomkins actually designates certain innate facial expressions, which he claims accompany eight or nine primary emotions. Whereas McDougall asserts that the different feelings[3] associated with the different emotions are caused by his central instinctual system, Tomkins borrows from James's theory (considered below) to postulate that the afferent feedback from these muscles, together with visceral disturbance, produces the experiential quality of the different emotions. Tomkins's theory is summarized in Figure 2.

While McDougall's theory has the advantage of focusing our attention on the directed, goal quality of different emotions, on the possibility that each emotion has an immediate motivational consequence, Tomkins's theory reminds us that emotional experience also feels good or bad in its own right. That is, quite apart from whether fear leads us to escape or love to approach, the experience of fear, love, or any other emotion may be pleasant or painful, acceptable or unacceptable in its own right. Besides any primary motivational consequences, there are definite secondary motivational conse-

---

[3] Throughout this monograph I shall use the term "feelings" to refer to the qualitative experience of the person who is having the emotion.

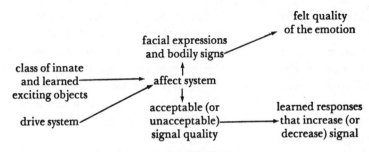

FIGURE 2. Tomkins's Theory

quences as a person seeks to obtain or avoid specific emotion feelings.

It seems clear that persons learn to anticipate having specific emotions if they perform given actions or let themselves get in certain situations. As Lazarus (1968) points out, we learn to control what emotions we will have. We may anticipate the negative or positive effects of getting angry or falling in love and we learn to avoid negative feelings—some of which, such as intense anxiety and shame, may be completely unacceptable. It is important to note that emotions may not only motivate by establishing goals of action but also, secondarily, by being sought after or avoided. In fact, as I have shown elsewhere (1968), even the most "rational" decisions, made coolly and without the influence of any direct emotion, are greatly influenced by the *anticipation* of emotion. For example, in deliberating whether or not to resist the invasion of South Korea, President Truman (1956) reports considering how he would feel about himself if he, as President, failed to resist the aggressive action of another nation.

Later we shall give more consideration to the role emotional experience plays in a person's life. Now, however, we shall turn to a third major effect of the emotions—their influence on the body. Some theorists regard this "expressive" aspect of emotion as the very basis of emotional experience.

James's Theory and Bodily Expression

In presenting his theory of the emotions, James states: "I now proceed to urge the vital point of my whole theory, which is this: *If we fancy some strong emotion, and then try to abstract from our consciousness of it all the feelings of its bodily symptoms, we find we have nothing left behind*, no 'mind-stuff' out of which the emotion can be constituted, and that a cold and neutral state of intellectual perception is all that remains. It is true that, although most people when asked say their introspection verifies this statement, some persist in saying theirs does not" (1890, p. 451).

Such observations led James to put forth his well-known theory that emotions are our perception of bodily changes—complex sensations stemming from the afferent feedback from our actions. James's theory is schematized in Figure 3.

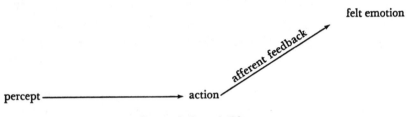

FIGURE 3. James's Theory

Bull (1951) has suggested that the theory be modified to include the attitude of the person. Before acting we must prepare our posture; we take a bodily attitude toward the object of the emotion. The proprioceptive feedback from this posture combines with visceral feedback to register as a conscious emotion. Bull states: ". . . from the present point of view, we feel angry as a result of the *readiness* to attack, and feel afraid as a result of *readiness* to run away, and not because of actually hitting out or running, as James explained the sequence" (p. 6).

Bull demonstrates that when emotions are evoked in hypnotized subjects definite postural reactions may be noted. For example, she reports that when fear is evoked there is a duality in the skeletal system and avertive movements exist simultaneously with a postural fixing of attention. In anger there is a primary tensing, forward-moving, attack response and a secondary restraining reaction.

There are numerous variations on the central idea that the experience of emotion stems from bodily feedback. Various investigations have emphasized feedback from the viscera, the cardiovascular system, the skeletal-postural muscles, and the facial muscles.[4] In fact, a skeptic might call this general theory the Hydra theory, for as soon as one hypothesis is disproved (as James's visceral hypothesis was by Cannon [1927]), other bodily systems are quickly proposed. Yet, in spite of the fact that it seems unlikely that bodily sensations are experienced as emotion, the general theory persists because it is clear that emotions can be influenced by bodily states.

A number of experiments have in fact demonstrated that the emotional states of at least some persons can be influenced by the injection of adrenalin (Schacter and Singer, 1962), by various drugs (Beck, 1967), or by the adoption of a muscular set (Laird, 1974). An important aspect of these experiments, and of natural observation, is that a person does not report experiencing an emotion if his bodily state is attributed to a drug or to a muscular posture. In such cases, he either reports no effect, or experiencing a state "as if" he were having an emotion. They argue convincingly that while the experience of an emotion includes some experience of the body and can be influenced by the state of the body, it is not sufficient simply to assert that emotional experience depends on the bodily state.

As a consequence, contemporary psychologists who emphasize the bodily component of emotional experience usually propose some additional ingredient in the existence of an emotion. Schacter and Singer (1962) propose that an emotion is also dependent on the person's cognition of his situation, Brenner (1974) argues that the emotion is a sensation of pleasure and/or unpleasure together with associated ideas, and Laird (1974) suggests that the emotion is a perception of what the person is doing (the bodily state providing cues that influence this percept).

Theorists who identify the experience of emotion with sensory feedback from the body may also emphasize the experiential quality of emotional behavior and its possible function as a

---

[4] A review of most of this work may be found in Izard (1971), who together with Tomkins emphasizes the facial muscles.

communicative device within a species. They cite the fact that ethologists have established the communicative function of behavioral displays and that at least a few human facial expressions (happiness, sadness, anger, disgust, and possibly fear and surprise) are reliably distinguished in many different cultures (Ekman, Sorenson, and Friesen, 1969; Izard, 1971).

On the other hand, the expressive quality of human emotion seems far more rich and variable than the rather stereotyped behavioral displays with which ethology deals. The fact that only a half dozen emotions have reliably discernible facial expressions stands in sharp contrast to the several hundred words designating emotions that exist in the English language. I would hypothesize that dozens of these terms can be reliably discerned by the average person and that dozens of emotional expressions can be reliably distinguished by trained observers who have situational and behavioral cues in addition to facial cues. In fact, the idea that we recognize emotions by responding to rather fixed facial expressions seems extremely atomistic. By contrast, Gestalt theory argues that we recognize emotional expressions because the expressive behavior reflects an organized structure—the same structure that underlies the experience of an emotion (Arnheim, 1949). For example, if subjects are asked to express emotions such as excitement or fury, they use straight lines broken by angles, whereas they represent sadness, laziness, or merriness by using curves (Lundholm, 1921).

Working within the framework of Gestalt theory, Arnheim (1958) has suggested that emotions are directly perceived in the same way that colors, shape, and movement are perceived. He argues that an attribute of any perception is its "directed tension"—e.g., the rising of notes in a scale, the upward thrust of a poplar tree, the progress of thought toward a goal, the yearning of a lover. This quality of directed tension is always present and underlies what we term either "expression" or "motivation." According to Arnheim, human expression and, more particularly, emotional expression is actually a special case of a much more general phenomenon. When we perceive the sadness of a weeping willow, we are not projecting our own sadness or seeing an analogy in the sense of thinking that the willow looks like a sad person. Rather, in such physiognomic perception, the directed tension inherent in the structure of the willow immediately conveys a quality of passive longing. In other words, it has the same pattern of directed tension that the emotion of sadness has; there is an isomorphism of form. Similarly, "weary" or "alert" movements reflect the directed tension inherent in the movements themselves, which often, in turn, reflect the directed tensions in the state of the person who is moving in a weary or an alert manner.

This approach to emotional expression may also be used to comprehend the effect the body may have on emotional experience. If a person assumes a particular posture whose kinesthetic structure of directed tensions is similar to those of a given emotional state, he will be inclined to experiencing that state. Note that this theory does not assume (as James's does) that the emotional experience *is* the kinesthetic sensation; rather the bodily posture is a component of emotion that reinforces or provokes the emotion as a whole because of the posture's structural similarity.[5] In any case, regardless of the extent to which emotional experience is constituted by afferent feedback from the body, James's theory and its contemporary derivatives remind us of the importance of the body in emotional experience and the fact that emotions are always *embodied*.

The Paulhan-Rapaport Model and Clinical Observation

Observing that we often become conscious of an emotion when our actions are blocked and there is a discrepancy between what actually exists and what we would like to exist, the French psychologist Paulhan postulates, *"An affect is the expression of a more or less profound disturbance of the organism, due to the fact that a relatively considerable quantity of nervous energy is released without being able to be used in a systematic manner"* (1884, p. 57).

---

[5] Similarly, the injection of adrenalin produces a stirred-up state that resonates with agitated emotions such as anger or hilarity (as Schacter and Singer demonstrated), but it may work against an experience of depression or contentment.

Many investigators have considered this view essentially correct and have expanded on it. After considering the writings of Freud, Federn, Whitehorn, and MacCurdy, Rapaport (1942) states: "Of the various theories, the following theory of the mechanism of emotions emerges as not conflicting with known facts: an incoming percept initiates an unconscious process which mobilizes unconscious instinctual energies; if no free pathway of activity is open for these energies—and this is the case when instinctual demands conflict—they find discharges through channels other than voluntary motility; these discharge processes—'emotional expression' and 'emotion felt'—may occur simultaneously or may succeed one another, or may occur alone. . ." (p. 37). These theoretical statements are schematized in Figure 4.

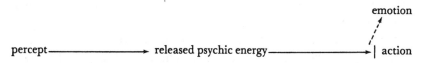

FIGURE 4. The Paulhan-Rapaport Model

According to this theory, when psychological energy cannot be used in action it manifests itself as conscious emotion or in emotional expressions such as visceral disturbances. As an individual develops, the ego learns to avoid being overwhelmed by the discharge of the energy and to use it instead as a signal that must be responded to.

While an energy model in general has a number of limitations (see Bowlby's critique, 1969, pp. 18-21) and while its application to emotion fails to distinguish anxiety from other emotions and does not account for some of the phenomena previously discussed, it does have the advantage of alerting us to a number of clinical phenomena and to the general problem of how a person deals with emotion. In an article on the clinical analysis of emotions, Schafer (1964) raises a number of questions that may be asked when we examine emotion in the context of a given individual's life. First, we may ask whether an emotion is currently present and experienced. We may know that a person is avoiding an emotion that we suspect would be beneficial for him to experience or, conversely, that the emotion he is experiencing has a histrionic quality or is being held onto so that we suspect it serves as a defense against some other more genuine emotion. In a related vein, we may ask whether the emotion is integrated with the person's life. Volkan (1976) distinguishes four different types of emotionality that occur within psychoanalytic treatment: (1) "blending emotions" where emotional experience blends with intellectual analysis to advance treatment; (2) "affectualization" where a superfluity of affect is used for defensive purposes; (3) "abreaction" where emotions attached to previously repressed experiences are blindly discharged but do not overwhelm the ego so that the patient may be assisted in forming a connection with the precipitating idea; and (4) "flooding" where no connection can be made by the patient between the affect and the event as the drive discharge is so great relative to the strength of the ego that all signal quality is lost.

From a somewhat different angle of inquiry, we may ask whether or not the person is aware of the event that actually precipitated the emotion—what he is really angry at, afraid of, or loving toward. And, more generally, we may inquire into the many different determinants that lead to the formation of a particular emotion at a particular time. In this regard we may wish to examine the internalized object relations that lead a person toward some emotions and away from others, the structuring of the ego with possible incorporations and splits, and whether the emotion is really the person's own, or whether it is borrowed from a significant other.

Finally, another line of inquiry suggested by Schafer relates character structure to how a person experiences and uses his emotions. One person may view his emotions as explosively dangerous yet precious, to be hoarded or given as presents, while another may make a display of his emotions. Conversely, the way in which a person relates to his emotions contributes to the shape of his personality. For example, Seton (1965) has described one patient who avoided experiencing his emotions as real by using a continual stream of histrionic emotions.

The very fact that we can ask such questions poses problems for all of the theories we have considered above, including the Paulhan-Rapaport model. If the emotions are as functional as McDougall and Tomkins suggest, how can we account for their many tortuous manifestations? On the other hand, if we consider emotions to be simple instinctual discharges (with or without signal properties), how can we account for the difference between real and spurious emotion and for the beneficial results when real emotion blends with intellectual insight? These questions lead to other types of theories.

EMOTION AND THE PERCEPTION OF VALUE

The concept of instinct (or any other bodily mechanism) suggests that emotions are rather mechanical affairs, and we have seen James propose that emotional experience is simple afferent feedback from the body. Such formulations hardly suggest that emotions relate to values. However, it is the same James who later wrote:

> Conceive yourself, if possible, suddenly stripped of all the emotion with which your world so inspires you, and try to imagine it *as it exists*, purely by itself, without your favorable or unfavorable, hopeful or apprehensive comment. It will be almost impossible for you to realize such a condition of negativity and deadness. No one portion of the universe would then have importance beyond another; and the whole collection of its things and series of its events would be without significance, character, expression, or perspective. Whatever of value, interest, or meaning our respective worlds may appear induced with are thus pure gifts of the spectator's mind. The passion of love is the most familiar and extreme example of this fact. If it comes, it comes; if it does not come, no process of reasoning can force it. Yet it transforms the value of the creature loved as utterly as the sunrise transforms Mont Blanc. . . . So with fear, with indignation, jealousy, ambition, worship. If they are there, life changes [1902, p. 150].

Whereas James sees emotion as transforming the world, others—from Plato through Ortega y Gasset—argue that emotion *reveals* what is valuable in the world. In either case, there is some relation between value and passion and this suggests that the moving force of emotion may stem from the perception of value rather than the impulse of instinct.

Arnold's Theory and the Appraisal of Value

In spite of the flexible connections between the environment and McDougall's instincts or Tomkins's affect signals, the emphasis is clearly on the environment controlling the person's behavior through a set of central mechanisms. Alternatively, we can speak of the person appraising the environment, with emotions resulting from the good or bad implications that an object has for the person. Arnold (1960) has summarized several such theories, which range historically from Aristotle's ideals to Michotte's experiments. She herself states: "As soon as we apprise something as worth having in an immediate and intuitive way, we feel an attraction toward it. As soon as we intuitively judge that something is threatening, we feel repelled from it, we feel urged to avoid it. The intuitive appraisal of the situation initiates an *action tendency that is felt as emotion*, expressed in various bodily changes, and that eventually may lead to overt action" (1960, p. 177). Her theory is summarized in Figure 5.

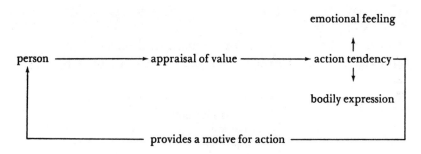

FIGURE 5. Arnold's Theory

While Arnold's action tendencies are similar to McDougall's instincts, it should be noted that they do not ordinarily lead directly to action, but rather serve as a motive for action if the person judges that the over-all benefits of the action will outweigh any negative effects. However, it seems to me that the major benefit of the theory is its insistence that emotions are not blind, mechanical processes but involve an active appraisal of the environment. Bowlby's (1969) account of the emotions follows Arnold closely but adds that the appraisal may also be of one's own states and impulses, and that the resulting emotions provide a monitoring service to oneself and a communicative service to others.

Angyal's Theory and Symbolization

One of the most neglected theories of the emotions has a number of interesting and original features. Angyal (1941) notes that an organism is constantly evaluating its situation and monitoring its significance for life processes. He proposes that the experience of an emotion is a symbol in the same sense that a perception is a symbol (e.g., when we see a "bird," our perception is an organized image with numerous features that have nothing to do with the retinal image). However, unlike perceptual or thought symbols, emotions are symbols for the welfare of the person in the situation in which he finds himself. Noting that Wundt (1897) distinguishes three dimensions of feeling states (pleasantness-unpleasantness, excitement-calming, and tension-relaxation), Angyal proposes that the quality of an emotion is determined both by the perception of value (which relates to the pleasantness-unpleasantness dimension) and by proprioceptive feedback from bodily responses (the qualities of excitement and tension) in the way James suggested. His theory is schematized in Figure 6.

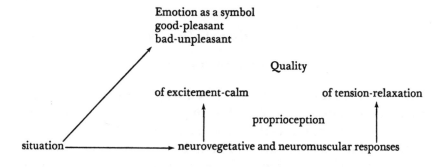

FIGURE 6. Angyal's Theory

Angyal is perhaps the only theorist who directly addresses the problem of why both passion and inspiration seem to come from outside the self. He suggests that the conscious self (which is only a part of the biological subject) tends to split off to establish its own government—a hegemony we call "will." Hence, when the remainder of the biological subject inevitably reasserts itself, the emotion appears to come from outside the ego. Together with Arnold, Angyal emphasizes the relation between evaluation and emotion. But perhaps the most salient feature of his theory is its insistence that an emotional experience must itself be symbolic—the product of active organization.

TRANSFORMATIONAL THEORIES

While value theories capture the fact that emotions reflect an appraisal and evaluation of the environment rather than the blind reaction to stimuli suggested by the instinct theories, they make emotion seem rather bland, lacking the imperative quality that emotions often have and which may be understood as an aspect of instinct. The various transformational theories attempt to explain the force of emotion as resulting from the changed position of the person relative to the world.

Sartre's Theory and the Magic of Emotion

While Paulhan and Rapaport postulate that emotion arises when instinctual energy is blocked, Sartre (1948) asserts that emotion occurs when a person discovers that he cannot act in the world in which he finds himself. Sartre suggests that when this happens, consciousness returns to a more primitive attitude and envisages itself in a magical world. The magical quality of emotional consciousness contrasts with our ordinary logical world, and is one of the basic ways in which consciousness exists (a mode in the same sense that sleeping or dreaming is a mode of consciousness). Thus, Sartre agrees with Freud that emotions, like dreams and hysteria, have the quality of primary-process thought. He simply insists that an emotion (or any other form of consciousness) is not a derivation of instinctual energy but is responsible for its mode of being-in-the-world.

Sartre suggests two basic classes of emotions. In one of these, the person, unable to achieve what he wants in the world by action, uses his body as an incantation to magically change the world. For example, in fear a person who is unable to escape may faint. Sartre contrasts flight with prudent withdrawal. He asserts "We do not flee in order to take shelter; we flee for lack of power to annihilate ourselves in the state of fainting" (p. 63). In the second class of emotions, the world itself is revealed as magical. This occurs particularly in the social world, which *is* a basically magical world. That is, try as we may, we keep viewing the behavior of others in a nondeterministic way (at least when we are close to them). For example, Sartre points out that we may be instantly horrified when a grinning face appears unexpectedly against our window. Here consciousness alters any aspect of the world that would reject the magical—for example, it disregards the panes of glass and yards of distance that stand between the face and the self. Sartre's theory is represented in Figure 7.

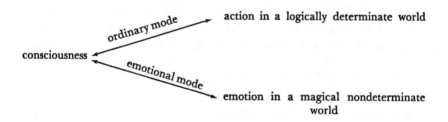

FIGURE 7. Sartre's Theory

Note that in Sartre's theory there is no unconscious part of the self that is manifested in phenomena such as èmotion. Rather, consciousness is always the basis of behavior; it simply manifests itself in different ways. One of these ways is the emotional mode of consciousness—a mode where the world is magical and consciousness manifests a type of primary-process thinking.

As Sartre emphasizes, when we experience emotion we are no longer so separated from objects in our world. The face that fills us with horror is not *out there*, separated from the self by distance and a window; it is experienced as *here*. Similarly, in anger, love, or any emotion, our relation to the object is transformed so that certain qualities of the object (or our self) become focal and the rest of the object and the world are forgotten. In fact, Dembo's (1976) experiments with anger suggest that there is a loosening of the boundaries that we ordinarily maintain between the self and the not-self and between reality and fantasy.

The same process appears to be involved in physiognomic perception where, in Arnheim's (1958) terms, the "directed tension" of an object is experienced in a personal way (e.g., seeing the "sorrow" of a teapot with a drooping spout). Indeed, qualities of objects such as "horrible," "majestic," and "enchanting" are both physiognomic and emotional. Koffka (1935) asserts that physiognomic qualities ". . . arise in objects when these objects are in dynamic relations with the Ego, when, otherwise expressed, a state of tension exists between them and the Ego. It is important to keep in mind that the kind of tension will vary for the different physiognomic characters. Not only will it be different in sign—positive or negative—and in degree, but also in quality. The kind of tension will determine our responses: attack, flight, approach, success, disregard, compassion, and so forth" (p. 362). He goes on to assert that the experience of physiognomic qualities implies an ego that is unified—but not merged—with its environment. This unification appears to be similar to what Dembo and Sartre are referring to when they speak of the boundary dissolution between self and environment that occurs with emotion.

Since the establishment of an ego boundary, with its separation of ego from the world, is a product of development, and since we associate merger and lack of distinction with psychotic states, the dissolution of the ego boundary is liable to be viewed as regressive. This seems unfortunate terminology. Although the formation of emotion *may* be regressive and reflect a merger, this is not an essential quality of emotion, which may be the result of *unification* rather than merger.

While developmental theory (Werner, 1940) draws a sharp distinction between *integration* (of differentiated parts) and merger (or diffuseness), it seems constantly to confuse the idea of *unification* and merger. This confusion arises because in both states there is a breakdown of differentiation, a "primitivization." However, in merger—a state of lesser development—there is either a failure to differentiate (the egocentricity a child manifests when it believes its mind is transparent to others) or a confusion of identity (the psychotic hallucinating a voice). As Modell (1968) argues, the lack of separation necessarily implies a lack of identity. In unification, this egocentricity or confusion and lack of identity is not always present. The person who experiences anger, love, or some other emotion is not necessarily being egocentric or confusing identities. Rather, he is insisting on a common reality that is shared between his self and the other—that there is something wrong to be angry about or something good to love. The differentiations that are dissolved in emotions are often false distinctions that have seemed to isolate, segregate, or otherwise disunify the self and the not-self. This may even be true when the emotion is serving a defensive purpose. Thus, in emotion per se the self/not-self distinction is not *erased* in the sense of there being egocentricity or confusion of identity. It is *dissolved* in the sense that a common reality is insisted upon so that a relationship replaces the segregation created by isolation of or incongruity between the self and the not-self.

The dissolution of the ego-other boundary also appears to be related to the loosening of the boundary between reality and unreality. Again, rather than leading to a psychotic-like confusion as to what is real and what is not, emotion enriches the imagination. This increase in imagination, associated with emotion, is a developmental *advance*. Hebb and Thompson (1954) indicate that the extent of emotionality demonstrated by members of a species is positively correlated with the size of the cortex. And Hillman (1961) interprets the literature on operations such as prefrontal lobotomy as showing that flattening of affect is closely related to loss of imagination.

Pribram's Theory and Neurological Models

It is interesting to note that there are a number of formal similarities between Sartre's theory, couched in the terms of phenomenological existentialism, and the neurophysiological model independently developed by Pribram and Melges (1969). While Sartre asserts that emotion occurs when we cannot act in the world, Pribram argues that emotions arise when the stimulus situation disequilibrates the neural system (the plan) that has organized behavior. In order to cope with this inability to act Sartre states that consciousness magically changes its world by emotion, while Pribram, analogously, suggests that the emotions reflect the operation of mechanisms designed to restore organization by regulating the *stimulus input* to the system (i.e., how the world is perceived). Finally, just as Sartre advances the idea that there are two broad classes of emotions—one of which makes the world magical, while the other adapts us to the magic of the world—Pribram proposes two types of emotions—one of which operates to adjust the stimulus input to conform to our plans, while the other adjusts our plans to conform to the stimulus input. Pribram's model is summarized in Figure 8.

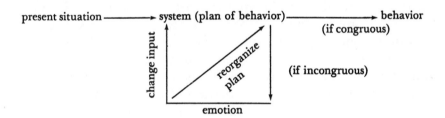

FIGURE 8. Pribram's Theory

Pribram's and Sartre's theories both belong to a general class of theories, which postulate that emotion occurs when the flow of action is prevented. However, there are different ways to conceptualize this inhibition. In the theories of Pribram and Sartre, action is blocked because it is incongruous with the situation the person perceives whereas in the Paulhan-Rapaport theory emotion arises when the flow of instinctual action is blocked—typically by conflict *within* the person. In fact, it may be argued that an inhibition of action is implicit in any choice situation. For example, Dewey (1895) suggests that no emotion is present as long as situations auto-

matically call forth either instinctual or habitual action patterns. However, if there is a choice of behavior and the organism is not sure which action will lead to the desired result,
action has to be inhibited until the best action can be selected.
He postulates that emotion reflects the tension inherent in this
conflict of selecting the correct action for the situation. This
whole class of theories in which emotion occurs when action is
inhibited contrasts with instinct theories such as McDougall's,
value theories such as Arnold's, or the transformational theory
we shall examine next, where the efficient cause of emotion is
a particular type of stimulus situation rather than the dis-
ruption of action.

Hillman's Theory and the Energy of Emotion

Working within a Jungian framework, Hillman (1961)
proposes that emotion is instigated when the unconscious and
the conscious self are joined by the occurrence of a symbol.
Since the unconscious is composed of instinctual forces with
their corresponding archetypal images, we might classify his
theory as an instinctual theory. However, in this theory
emotion is not simply an expression of instinct, it is the joining
together of the instinctual unconscious with the conscious self
and thus an activity of the psyche as a whole. Furthermore,
this union results in a transformation of the self—a reorgani-
zation that is necessarily beneficial unless the conscious self is
not strong enough to handle the force of the unconscious.
(Phenomena such as acting out or histrionic emotion are not
the products of such a union and, hence, are neither true
emotion nor beneficial.) Of equal theoretical importance, this
transformation of the self, the heart of emotion, is postulated
to be a transformation of *energy*. Hillman's theory is schematized in Figure 9.

While the concept of energy is implicit in McDougall's
theory and explicit in the Paulhan-Rapaport theory, such instinctual energy is usually conceived as a special type of biological or psychic energy that differs from physical energy.
There are a number of arguments against such a conceptualization: The dualism seems unsound, and the instinctual

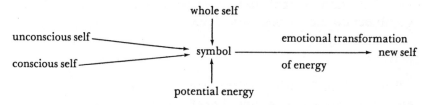

F<small>IGURE</small> 9. Hillman's Theory

energy does not lend itself to measurement and is not always conserved in the manner of physical energy. However, the energy conceptualized by Hillman is a general energy (analogous to that of Whitehead [1938]), which may either be revealed as physical energy or as psychological energy. Emotion is said to be "the psychological aspect of general energy." In such a conception, the physical world is seen to have an emotional aspect, which is reflected, for example, in its having value and meaning, and which may be affected by a person's emotion. This general energy is often stored in the body's posture, in its habits, or in the momentum of a human relationship, etc., but is released as kinetic energy—in the form of emotional experience and behavior, a transformation of the self—by the occurrence of a symbol.

While such a conceptualization may have heuristic value, particularly for those inclined to an intuitive approach, its scientific value seems to depend ultimately on the ability to measure successfully the psychological aspect of general energy. For our present purposes, it serves the useful function of reminding us of the energic aspect of emotionality. For regardless of whether we *conceptualize* emotions as a form of energy or as a set of instructions or blueprints, as a feedback mechanism or as a complex of sensations, emotions may be *experienced* as having an energic presence that is expressed by the body. On the one hand, the flow of this emotional energy may be felt as life fulfilling, in contrast to the deadness that seems present when a person avoids his emotions. On the other hand, emotions may be experienced as overwhelming and disorganizing, the person feeling unable to handle the intensity of the energy he experiences. This experience of the

energy of emotion seems to be related to the dissolution of the
ego-object boundary mentioned above.[6]

SUMMARY

Rather than focusing on the conflicting nature of the different theories, let us assume that they each accurately portray
different aspects of emotion. We may summarize as follows:

1. Each emotion provides an impetus to act in a specified
way (McDougall).

2. The experience of the emotion may act as a secondary
motive, with the person seeking to attain or avoid the emotion
(Tomkins).

3. Emotions are always embodied. They both influence the
body, being expressed in its state and movement, and reflect
the condition of the body and the form of its behavior (James).

4. Emotions may overwhelm a person or be used by him,
reflect disintegration or promote integration (Paulhan-Rapaport).

5. Emotions are closely related to the appraisal of value
(Arnold).

6. The experience of an emotion is itself an organization in
the same sense that perception is an organization (Angyal).

7. Emotional experience involves a dissolution of the ego-
object boundary that transforms our perception of the world
(Sartre).

8. Emotions involve the transformation of energy in that the
potential energy stored in posture, habits, attachments, etc.,
is released in a way that unifies the self (Hillman).

It is unclear whether emotions result when our action is
blocked (Paulhan, Rapaport, Sartre, Pribram), when a stimulus situation requires or leads to action (McDougall, Tomkins,
James, Arnold), or when unconscious aspects of the self come
into contrast with consciousness (Angyal, Hillman).

---

[6] While the concept of boundary dissolution primarily refers to how the
person perceives the world when he experiences emotion, the perceptual
transformation emphasized by Sartre seems closely bound to the energic
transformation emphasized by Hillman.

A Sketch of the Structural Theory

Any attempt to create a new theory of the emotions by simply synthesizing these different aspects of emotion would have about as much success as attempting to portray an elephant from the accurate but misleading description of its parts. Instead, I propose that we return to examine the *movement* of emotion that all the theories attempt to explain. I shall temporarily abandon the search for a general theory of emotional movement and concentrate instead on the movement of the various individual emotions. There is an important reason for this strategic retreat: while all theorists attempt to tackle "emotion," in fact they focus on some particular emotion or set of emotions that is of especial personal interest. Rapaport tends to focus on anxiety; McDougall on anger, fear, and other emotions whose conative impulses seem clear; Tomkins on eight emotions with clear facial expressions; James on those where bodily disturbance is involved, etc. They then assume that this emotion or set of emotions is typical and generalize their theory to emotion. Such a theory is very resistant to change because anything that doesn't fit is not really an emotion! To guard against this tendency we shall examine the full range of emotions named in the English language.

A description of the different movements of the emotions is a necessary foundation for the actual construction of the theory I shall propose. But before beginning such a construction, it is helpful to look at an over-all sketch of the theory so that we have some general idea of what is being constructed and do not become lost in the important parts which compose the whole. Such a sketch is necessarily abstract and its full meaning will only become apparent as we proceed to construct the theory by examining particular emotions. With this caution, we may outline the theory as follows.

The experience of emotion reflects the *transformation* of our relation to the world — to the persons, objects, events, and actions that are important to us. These transformations are the movements of emotion and each type of emotion (anger, fear, love) reflects a different kind of transformation. A trans-

formation is not a passive reaction to a given stimulus situation, rather it is a *transaction* between the person and his environment, a way of organizing the relation between the
person and the other so that the response itself gives meaning
to the stimulus situation—e.g., "a hole is to dig."

These organizations, or ways to transform object relations,
are not isolated mechanisms. Rather, they are related to each
other in a way that permits a person to unconsciously "choose"
how he will organize his relation to the situation in which he
finds himself. In one sense the person is free to choose any of
the organizations available to him. However, as we shall see,
once an organization is chosen, an entire network of other
relations is determined. In a real sense then a person's
emotional freedom lies in the recognition of the necessities
attendant on any choice.

Since the organization of each different emotion (each way
of transforming the person's relation to his environment) is
related to every other emotion in a specifiable way, we are
really dealing with a *structure* of emotions. That is, while
individual emotions each have an identity, they are not separate entities but are parts of a whole—a system that governs
object relations or a "structure." I am using "structure" here
in Piaget's (1970) sense. He states: "As a first approximation,
we may say that a structure is a system of transformations.
Inasmuch as it is a system and not a mere collection of elements and their properties, these transformations involve
laws: the structure is preserved or enriched by the interplay of
its transformation laws, which never yield results external to
the system nor employ elements that are external to it. In
short, the notion of structure is comprised of three key ideas:
the idea of wholeness, the idea of transformation, and the idea
of self-regulation" (p. 5).

The major details of an over-all structure of the emotions
will be outlined in the next chapter where we shall see that the
different movements or transformations of the emotions can
be related to each other in a systematic way so that each different emotion has a place in an over-all structure of which it
is a part. We shall find that the way in which this structure is
organized suggests that it is designed to govern object relations

(the relation between the person and his environment) and that the most parsimonious explanation suggests the basic unit of emotional analysis is the dyad (the person and the other) rather than the individual. That is, we shall be forced to conclude that at the very beginning of his development a person is organized so that both "he" and the "other" are in a dynamic relationship. We shall also find that there are several different dimensions to the psychological space in which movement can occur and that many states that might not be considered to be emotions (e.g., calmness and appreciation) are emotions in that they participate in the over-all structure we shall describe.

By the end of the second chapter, then, it should be evident that the various emotions may be conceived of as parts of an overall structure. However, there is a danger that the concrete details of the individual emotions may get lost in the elegance of this abstract forest. To guard against too great a departure from the concrete, in Chapter Three we shall return to an individual emotion and examine its movement in greater detail. We shall find that it is possible to describe each emotion's transformation in considerable detail. In fact, each emotion may be said to have its own substructure. There is a definite structure to the situation in which the emotion occurs, the emotion acts to transform this situation (always an object relation) in a particular way, and this transformation serves a definite function involving the preservation or development of the person's object relations.

In the concluding chapter we shall examine the extent to which the theory can account for the different aspects of emotion emphasized by the theories examined above. We shall attempt to quantify the power of the theory to discriminate between all the various emotions that exist. Finally, we shall discuss whether the proposed structure of the emotions is "real" or if it has been imposed on the data, and indicate the various aspects of the theory that may be verified or disproved by future investigation.

Chapter Two

THE MOVEMENTS
OF THE EMOTIONS

When we turn to particular emotions to examine the nature of the movement that each manifests, we encounter the fact that the English language has hundreds of words referring to emotional states. Davitz (1969) reports that a scanning of *Roget's Thesaurus* yields over 400 words that may be used as labels for emotional states, and that 137 of these were selected by over half of his 40 subjects as terms they would personally use.[1] If we examine the literature on the emotions, we find that some 247 different terms have been used by those theorists who have presented some listing of the emotions and that at least 154 of these are judged to be emotions by contemporary laypersons (see Appendix C). Thus, depending on exactly what is considered to be an emotion, we have between 100 and 500 words, which presumably capture different nuances of emotion. To this list, we might add a number of words in other languages for which there is no English equivalent. We might also consider metaphors, which capture various shades of meaning that are missed by single words.

Rather than becoming disheartened by the immensity of this terminology, I propose that we make good use of it and begin to analyze the different emotions suggested by these terms. After all, hundreds of thousands of organic compounds have been discovered and it has proved very profitable to

[1] Unfortunately, only 50 of these words "chosen on an intuitive basis" are reported.

38

describe their various structures. However, we would be overwhelmed if we attempted to master hundreds of emotions right away. I suggest that we begin with one emotion, contrast it with another, contrast these two with two more, and thus gradually build up an understanding of the structure of all the emotions. We could begin with any emotion, our results being independent of the starting place. I shall begin with the emotion of anger.

What is the basic movement of anger? Clearly, it is against the object toward which the anger is directed. The person who is angry wants to hurt, destroy, remove, or change the object. He may attempt to withdraw from his anger. He may smolder, sulk, or become passively aggressive. But these forms of behavior cannot relieve the anger itself, which is directed toward the end of moving the object away from the self.

Let us contrast anger with fear. In the latter, the self moves away from the object that is feared. Rather than altering the position of the object, the subject alters his own position. Although to accomplish this end the person may have to control himself and may even approach the object and destroy it, the way in which the object is approached betrays the basic fear, and there is no pleasure in the destruction, only a relief.

Now let us contrast these movements with emotions that involve a genuine approach. Here we ordinarily say the movement is toward the object. But let us be careful. The fact that we distinguish between two ways of increasing distance (moving against and moving away) suggests that there may also be two ways of decreasing distance—two ways of moving toward. In fact many theorists have suggested basic distinctions in how we approach another. For example, Ortega y Gasset (1957) points out that the emotion of desire involves a centripetal force that demands possession of the object and brings the other toward us, while the centrifugal force of erotic love takes us out of ourselves in a movement that goes toward the other. D'Arcy (1956) distinguishes two components of human love—a self-centered desire to possess and an other-centered desire to surrender. And Fromm (1956) separates agape, a disinterested love toward all, from eros, a demand for union with a beloved.

POSITION ALTERATION

As a basic theoretical postulate, I shall assume that we may meaningfully contrast two basic forms of approach movements and that this contrast corresponds to the contrast between anger and fear. Thus, I shall distinguish a positive movement toward the other that alters the position of the self from a positive movement toward the other that brings the other toward the self. The former is illustrated in emotions such as affection, devotion, and tenderness, where one's "heart goes out to the other." The latter is reflected in emotions such as desire, fascination, and longing, where one wants the other for one's self.

It is intriguing that the distinction between these four basic relations may be captured by different bodily movments of extension and contraction. If the arms are held out in a circle so that the finger tips almost touch, they may either be brought toward the body (a movement of contraction) or moved out in an extension. The entire trunk may follow these movements. Now if the palms are facing in, the extension movement corresponds to a moving toward the other—a giving—as in tenderness, while the contraction movement suggests a movement toward the self—a getting—as in longing. If the palms are rotated out, the extension movement corresponds to the thrusting against of anger, while the contraction intimates the withdrawal away of fear. The reader may wish to experiment with these four basic movements. If one allows oneself to become involved in the movement and imagines an object, one may experience the corresponding emotion. The distinctions drawn thus far are summarized in Table 1.

At this point we must digress for just a moment in order to consider some issues of semantics. The various words that "name" emotions often have several different usages and of course even in a particular usage the word itself is not an emotion. Therefore, in using "emotion names" in this monograph, I have two different problems. On the one hand, I use each of these words in a very particular sense. When I use the term "desire," I use it to represent a particular type of emo-

TABLE 1
FOUR BASIC EMOTIONAL MOVEMENTS

Movement of Person	Bodily Movement	Typical Emotion
Toward other	+ extension	Love
Toward self	+ contraction	Desire
Away from self (against other)	− extension	Anger
Away from other	− contraction	Fear

tion—the type we experience when we want to have a person or object for ourselves. I do not use it in its sense as a general sort of impulse—as when the angry person desires to hit or the scared person desires to run. Similarly, I use the term "love" to refer only to a particular emotion characterized by giving—a movement toward the other—rather than to the sentiment of "love" that involves the entire cluster of both giving and getting emotions—movements both toward the other and toward the self. On the other hand, I do not use these terms arbitrarily, but to refer to an emotion that I assume is also known to the reader. I am interested in the emotion itself rather than its name, and I use the terms simply as a way to refer to the emotion. As Buytendijk (1950) remarks, "In daily life as well as in science a word generally functions like a chain to get hold of a dog, to have the dog near us, and to do with it what we like. The phenomenologist, however, is not interested in the chain but in the dog itself" (p. 140). By being careful of word usage, I hope to insure that we are examining similar experiences; once that is assured the reader may agree or disagree with my description of the experience.

Returning to Table 1, it may be noted that the four basic movements we have described affect the person's relation with the other and, in fact, correspond to four basic modes of object relation: giving, getting, removing, and escaping. Rather than conceiving of emotions as simple reactions to stimuli—responses that are automatically discharged—we may view emotions as "instructions" which tell the organism

how to behave in relation to its stimulus situation.[2] Depending
on the strength of the emotion, these instructions range from
the merest hints to overpowering imperatives. Thus, instead of
viewing emotions as either reflexes or as instrumental behavior
(the means to an end), we may see them as establishing their
own ends—of giving to, getting, removing, or escaping from
the other—ends that relate the person to the environment.

Such a conceptualization raises an interesting question: how
many distinctive instructions might we expect? Psychology as a
whole has emphasized only one basic distinction—that
between positive and negative. We have Lewin's concept of
positive and negative valence (the quality of objects that leads
us to approach or avoid them), Skinner's positive and negative
reinforcers (stimuli whose appearance or disappearance
increases the probability of the preceding behavior), and
Freud's life and death instincts (the processes involved in the
building up and tearing down of units). We might therefore
expect to find only two basic types of emotional movement—
decreasing and increasing the distance between the person
and the other. Yet we have already discerned four types of
movement. Either this reflects the fact that emotions are
simply isolated patterns of behavior, in which case the most we
can hope to achieve is a descriptive list of unrelated response
tendencies, or that the different emotions are parts of some
system that involves at least one other fundamental distinction
besides positive and negative.

Our first postulate, that we may meaningfully contrast two
basic forms of both positive and negative movement, implies
that there is another fundamental distinction we must make.
This distinction is related to whether emotional movement is
oriented to moving an other toward or away from the self
(whose position remains constant) or moving the self toward or
away from the other. It would be surprising if such a
fundamental distinction were not reflected in the theories of at

---

[2] After examining Watson's report of the different stimuli that elicit fear, rage,
and love, and the responses that characterize these emotions. Tolman concludes:
"It is not a response *as such*, nor a stimulus situation, *as such*, that constitute the
behavioral definition of an emotion, but rather the response as affecting or calculated to affect the stimulus situation" (1923, p. 223).

least some psychologists and, in fact, I believe related distinctions may be found in the work of Angyal (1941) and Piaget (1971). The former draws a basic distinction between two developmental trends that complement rather than oppose each other. One of these is a trend toward "autonomy" — the self expanding its sphere of independence and its control over the environment; the other is toward "homonomy" — the self becoming a part of enterprises that are larger than itself.

In a rather different vein, Piaget describes development as the result of two complementary processes: assimilation and accommodation. In the former, the data are given a meaning that is in accord with the schemata that already exist; thus, the world is incorporated into the self. In the latter, the data force a change in the existing schemata and the self accommodates to the world. It seems to me that the trend toward autonomy and the process of assimilation involve a basic orientation toward the self and its expansion, while the trend toward homonomy and the process of accommodation involve an orientation toward the other as existing apart from the self.

BELONGING

If the distinction described above and the positive-negative distinction are fundamental aspects of object relations and if the different emotions may be conceived of as parts of one system that instruct a person as to how he should relate to another, it would be useful to find a single concept flexible enough to capture the distinctions and instructions we have described. The concept of *belonging* seems to fulfill this function. That is, we may say that the movement toward the other, the instruction to give, which is characteristic of love, is equivalent to a transformation of the person's relations to the other so that the person "belongs" to the other in the sense that the person makes the other's concerns his own. Then the movement toward the self which is characteristic of desire is the equivalent of the person wanting the other to belong to the self—to "be mine"—to have the other involved in the concerns of one's self.

Conversely, the movement of anger away from the self is the equivalent of "don't be mine," "I do not want you to belong to me," "remove the other." And fear's movement away from the other involves a basic feeling that one should not belong to the other—i.e., "don't be possessed by that other," "don't make his interests yours." In the next chapter we shall find that a change in the relation of belonging and the different movements or instructions that characterize the different emotions actually involves a set of transformations in a number of relations between the person and the objects of his environment, transformations which affect the self, the body, and the other, as well as one's basic relation to the world. However, for our present purposes we may simply characterize these transformations as involving the relation of belonging. The four major transformations are summarized in Table 2.

TABLE 2
FOUR BASIC EMOTIONAL TRANSFORMATIONS

Emotion	Movement of Person	Instruction	Transformation
Love	Toward other	Give	Self belongs to other
Desire	Toward self	Get	Other belongs to self
Anger	Away from self	Remove	Other does not belong to self
Fear	Away from other	Escape	Self does not belong to other

THE SUBJECT AND OBJECT OF THE EMOTION

It should be noted that in all four of the emotions described, regardless of whether there is an orientation toward or away from the other or the self, the person is the subject of a movement that is directed at an other who is a clear object. We may contrast such emotions with a set of affects where there is no apparent other and the object of the affect seems to be the person's self—states such as depression, anxiety, confidence, and security.

Are such states of mind emotions? Persons committed to an activation theory of the emotions might only include anxiety as an emotion; our list of terms classified as emotions by previous theorists also includes confidence and depression, but omits security. Clearly, the answer depends on our implicit theory of the emotions, on what we conceive emotions to be. The theory advanced here holds that an emotion exists whenever a person is moved—whenever his relation to the world is transformed. Since a person is transformed if he becomes depressed or if he becomes secure, I shall include these states as emotions. For simplicity we may term these emotions, where the self is the object of the movement, "me" emotions, in contrast to the "it" emotions, which have an other as object and whose movements we have already examined.[3] From the perspective of this approach, even calmness, the antithesis of what many could call an emotion, is considered an emotion, provided that calmness does not refer to some affectless state, but rather to the implicit transformation involved when a person is calm in spite of a demanding situation. That is, we would expect the person to be disturbed were he not calm—transformed by his inner strength of character. If the person is calm but no transformation is involved, the person is simply out of touch with the demands of the situation.

Let us examine the movements inherent in these me emotions. In depression, there is a clear movement away from the world as the person loses interest in objects and finds that the self is no longer able to will—to imagine and carry out actions in the world. In the next chapter we shall see that in the case of situational depressions this loss of will involves giving up a position that is untenable. The loss is functional in the sense that it protects the self from the injury that would

---

[3] An it emotion may be directed at the self—may have the self as its "other"—as when a person is angry at himself. However, here the self is being treated as an objective other would be. Conversely one may feel depressed at an other's behavior, but only if the other is part of one's self and thus the self is really the object of the movement.

occur if the person acted in the way he believes he ought to act.

The constriction of depression contrasts sharply with the positive expansion inherent in confidence or euphoria where the person is interested in the world, moves out in it, and feels able to act effectively. The emotion of confidence functions to enable a person to assert his own particular view of reality. For example, in Asch's (1951) experiment on conformity pressure, a person's judgment as to which of two lines is longer is challenged by others who have been secretly instructed to disagree. In spite of the fact that the person's judgment is objectively correct, only those persons with confidence are able to continue asserting their personal view without becoming rigid or anxious. A similar process is often involved in making important decisions. For example, at the beginning of the Korean War, the North Korean invasion forced American troops to the southern tip of South Korea. When reinforcements became available, General MacArthur believed that the best strategy was to make an amphibious landing at the port of Inchon, far behind the bulk of the North Korean forces. He reasoned that this would cut supply lines and force a two-front war, whereas a simple frontal assault would cost many more lives. The problem with his vision was the extreme risks involved (enormous tides, mines, shore batteries, etc.) and, because of this, the Joint Chiefs of Staff came to Tokyo to dissuade MacArthur and suggest an alternative. There is little doubt that most persons would have lacked the strength to maintain their vision and assert it in the face of such strong opposition. Elsewhere (de Rivera, 1968, pp. 175-179) I have reviewed the risks involved and how MacArthur's confidence enabled him to convince the Joint Chiefs of Staff without blinding himself as to the risks. In fact, the landing proved to be completely successful.

The "giving up" of depression and "taking hold" of confidence contrast sharply with the "letting go" of security. The secure child can let go of his mother to explore a new place, the secure adult can let go of his position in an argument to examine the position held by the other. In contrast to confidence and the assertion of reality, the emotion of security functions to enable a person to surrender his (willed) view of reality and abandon himself to new and different perspectives. Wolff (1964) has described this process of "surrender" and how the person later evaluates his "catch" of new information. This ability to give up a vision of reality is especially important when a person who has committed himself to a particular view receives information that indicates he is wrong. As Kelly (1965) has written, such information poses a serious threat and often provokes hostility in an attempt to extort confirming evidence. In order to be open to such contradictory evidence, one must possess security or be in a secure position. Such security permits openness when the stakes are high and enables a person to let things be rather than trying to force a solution by rigid imposition of will. Goldstein (1951) has described how this is essential for abstract thinking to occur. Similarly, when one might be ridiculed or slighted, security enables one to be oneself without creating the phony sort of "presentation of self" that Goffman (1959) often describes. And, of course, it is security that enables a lover to abandon himself and cope with the potential threat that merger may pose for his identity. It should be noted that while security enables one to accommodate and accept the reality of others and to admit that one may be wrong, confidence permits assimilation and the ability to assert one's own reality and to believe that one is right.

To some extent one can trade off confidence and security. Thus, in order for a person to be able to commit himself to anything (a viewpoint, a goal, a person, etc.), he must *either* be confident enough to know that he is right *or* secure enough not to mind if he is wrong. But when the commitment is in error, only security can provide openness (just as when the situation is unclear, only confidence can provide decisiveness).

All the above movements may be contrasted with that of anxiety. The movement of anxiety is opposite to that of security just as the movement of confidence is opposite to that of depression. The emotion of anxiety involves a defensive clinging to one's current reality, a "holding on" to the parent, to one's group, or to whatever provides the defenses that are required when the conditions of security are absent.

48   JOSEPH DE RIVERA

These movements and the corresponding instructions are
summarized in Table 3.

We may now inquire as to whether there may be a relation
between these emotions whose object is the self and those emotions, previously considered, whose object is an other. We
have noted that the former have no *apparent* other, but let us
examine the matter more closely.

TABLE 3
BASIC MOVEMENTS OF FOUR ME EMOTIONS

Emotion	Basic Movement	Instruction
Security	Surrendering—allowing world to come into self	Let go
Confidence	Expanding self into world	Take hold
Depression	Constricting self away from world	Give up
Anxiety	Defending—keeping world out of self	Hold on

We are familiar with a number of links between the two sets
of emotions: some security seems necessary in order for a
person to love and we know that the secure child has a loving
parent; anxiety often seems to be a consequence of what is
perceived to be parental withdrawal; confidence may stem
from being wanted; and the depressed person may erupt in
violent anger which may have been directed against a part of
himself. May it be that there is an other who is implicit in each
of the emotions, an other who is moving in relation to the self,
who has the self as an object? I shall postulate that this is so,
that in each of the emotions where the self is the object of the
emotion, the self is the object for the movements of an implicit
other.[4]

[4] As Dahl (see p. 6) suggests, such a conceptualization is related to the Freudian
conception of internalization. Hence it may possibly serve as a link between
psychoanalytic thought and the ideas of George Herbert Mead and the symbolic
interactionists.

We may assume that the movements of the implicit other are the same movements we have already described as inherent in the other-directed emotions. That is, when the self is the object of the emotion, the implicit other is either moving toward or away from the self or moving the self toward or away from it (the other). Indeed, these movements seem to be reflected in the bodily posture of the person having the emotion. The depressed person is almost literally pressed down, exactly as if he were on the receiving end of the negative extension movement of an angry other. Similarly, the person who is confident is puffed out—the chest extended, the head high—his expansion revealing the "pull" of an other who desires him. The postures of anxiety and security are not so obviously related to the movements of another. However, it is not difficult to imagine that the open, free movement of the person who is secure and the tense, rigid movements of the anxious person are related to the positive extension or negative contraction of an implicit other.

Since we assume that these interrelations are all part of one system, they may be best understood by again referring to the concept of belonging. We may then analyze the self-as-object emotions as follows: The secure person feels that his parent (or significant other) belongs to (i.e., loves) him. As Bowlby (1969) shows, the secure child knows that the parent is there for him and can thus venture away. Similarly, the secure adult can explore new realities and can let events occur without having to control their outcome. These new experiences allow the world to enter the self and inevitably lead the person toward a new self and separation from the other. The experience of security instructs a person to "let go"—to venture forth and allow change to occur—that it will be all right because the implicit other will still belong to him.

Anxiety occurs when the implicit other withdraws his belonging to the person. That is, the implicit other is sensed as experiencing the same "don't belong to that" that is inherent in fear. Such withdrawal may occur initially, as Sullivan (1953) suggests, when the infant behaves in a manner that is unacceptable to the parent. Later the experience of anxiety occurs when the person considers accepting responsibility for actions and emotions that would lead to an identity that, he believes, would occasion withdrawal of the other. The anxiety essentially instructs the person to deny this responsibility, to say "that isn't me," and thus hold on to the old self and relationship whose abandonment is threatened. While this moves the person away from a new identity, it defends him against a loss of belonging to the other.

Confidence exists when the implicit other wants the self to belong to it. The person knows that he — and the reality he asserts — is desirable. Just as a secure character structure develops out of parental love, I believe a confident character structure develops from parental desire for the child. While one case hardly constitutes proof of this assertion, it is interesting to observe the relationship between MacArthur (whose degree of confidence has already been described) and his mother. At one point in his career the future General was in danger of being expelled from West Point for refusing to divulge the name of a suspected cadet. His mother wrote him a poem encouraging him to stick to his guns. The first two lines read:

> Do you know that your soul is of my soul such a part,
> That you seem to be fiber and core of my heart?
> [MacArthur, 1964, p. 25].

Depression occurs when the implicit other moves against the self — "you don't belong to me." Note that the loss here is not really a withdrawal of the other's love but a loss of the other's desire to possess one's own love, and the consequent narcissistic injury or devaluation of the self. The emotion instructs the person not to act and to constrict the self. Sullivan (1956) has shown that in cases of actual loss, the grief reaction or abandoning of attachment to the other (relinquishing them as part of the self) is necessary for the person to continue functioning in reality. In Chapter Three we shall see that the depressive reaction — the loss of the will to act — is also necessary in certain circumstances and serves a definite function.

The transformations linking the me emotions to the movements of the it emotions are summarized in Table 4.

TABLE 4
TRANSFORMATIONS RELATING IT AND ME EMOTIONS

It Emotion	Transformation	Person Moves	Corresponding Me Emotion	Other Moves	Transformation
Love	Self belongs to other	Toward other	Security	Toward person	Other wants to belong to person
Desire	Other belongs to self	Other toward self	Confidence	Person toward other	Other wants person to belong to other
Anger	Other does not belong to self	Other away from self	Depression	Person away	Other wants person to belong to self
Fear	Self does not belong to other	Away from other	Anxiety	Away from person	Other wants not to belong to person

As Table 4 makes apparent, each self-directed or me emotion is paired with an object-directed, it emotion in such a way that the movement directed at the self by the object implicit in the me emotion mirrors the movement of the self in the paired it emotion. In fact, our second postulate implies that this is so for *all* emotions. That is, every me emotion will be paired with a corresponding it emotion and vice versa. To verify this conclusion we must look at another set of emotions and determine whether or not they too may be divided into emotions with an object and emotions with the self as object, and whether or not the movements of each me emotion seem to mirror a corresponding it emotion.

Thus far we have been concerned with a set of emotions connected to transformations in a relation that I have called belonging. Rather than attempting a precise definition of this term, I have relied on our intuitive understanding of the relation. However, I want to specify certain features of this relation so that we may contrast it with other relations. First, belonging implies a *boundary* between what belongs and what does not belong. It is this property of belonging that James (1890) uses when he distinguishes and defines the self as "everything that can be called mine."[5] Second, belonging implies a *connection* between the person and the other (or whatever belongs). While this connection may be a logical one (e.g., a part necessarily belongs to the whole), it is a *binding* connection. When we speak of the person as belonging to an other we imply that he has made the other's concerns his own to the extent that he will feel gladdened by the other's gains

---

[5] The concept of belonging is the principal undefined concept of set theory where the elements of a set are said to belong to the set. In this terminology we may say that the emotions of desire and anger involve possession in the sense that the person is the set and wants the other (as an element of the set) to belong to the person (desire) or to not belong to the person (anger). In the corresponding me emotions of confidence and depression, it is the other who wants to belong or not belong to the person (who is still the set). The emotions of love and fear have to do with belonging in the sense that the other is the set and the person an element who wants to belong to the other (love) or not to belong to the other (fear). In the corresponding me emotions of security and anxiety, it is the other who wants the person (still an element) to belong or not belong to the set. While in confidence the self contains everything, in security it is contained as part of a larger whole.

and saddened by the other's pain. Similarly, when we speak of something as belonging we expect that the person will have a personal interest in the belonging—whether it be a part of his body, a cherished possession, or a member of his family—as the object literally becomes part of the self and the person mourns any loss of this connection. This aspect of the self is what James called the "material" self.

RECOGNITION

Now let us examine another fundamental human relation—*recognition*. The concept of recognizing, like that of belonging, is rich with implications. On the one hand, to recognize means to identify, to know again; on the other hand, it means to acknowledge a person as a member of a special group, to honor or admit to some privileged status. In defining recognition as an emotional relation, we shall see that these diverse meanings are united.

For our purpose, to explicate a system of emotional relations, we would like to be able to discover an entire set of emotions that regulate recognition rather than belonging yet that correspond to the latter set in a one to one fashion in that both sets of emotions have identical movements toward or away, from the other or the self. Such a set is illustrated in Table 5.

Note that the emotions governing recognition are concerned with what the other is like, with how he appears in the eyes of others. These emotions deal with what James (1890) called the "social" self—the self as recognized by the other—and involve one's honor, reputation, and morality. This concept embraces both the self-image and the ideal self for both can only be validated by an other. While, in a strict sense, there are as many social selves as there are others who know us,[6] the most important others are those whom we love, and one of our major concerns involves maintaining our self in their eyes. It might be objected that an inner-directed person

---

[6] Mead (1934) suggested that we might speak of a "generalized other."

TABLE 5
A SET OF FOUR RECOGNITION EMOTIONS

Movement	Emotions	
Person Moves	Governing Belonging	Governing Recognition
Toward other	Love	Esteem
Toward self	Desire	Admiration
Away from self	Anger	Contempt
Away from other	Fear	Horror

is only concerned with maintaining his own self-concept. However, even our most private self—the "real" self that no one else can fully see—must be an essentially social reality (be potentially recognized by an other). In fact, James suggests that the reason most persons pray to God is that they must conceive of *some* other who can recognize their self for what it, in its ultimate loneliness, truly is.

Let us examine the movements of each of the emotions concerned with recognition of the other. The emotion of esteem essentially involves recognizing the other as one who acts in accord with the moral imperatives that his position requires of him. We recognize him as a person who upholds the shared values that make us part of the same group. Hence, esteem involves recognizing the other not only in the sense of giving him honor, but also in the sense of recognizing the other as a member of our group—whether that be a profession, a nation, or humanity. The person whom we esteem is an ideal member of our group and reflects the values that we ideally expect from all its members.

At first glance it might seem that admiration involves the same movement as esteem, for both involve a positive regard for the other. However, just as we drew a distinction between two types of positive belonging—depending on whether the person wanted to belong to the other or have the other belong to himself—we may distinguish between esteem, as a recognition of the other for himself, and admiration, as a recognition of the ideal self in the other. When we closely examine the emotion of admiration, we find that the person whom we admire inevitably possesses qualities we want for ourselves, qualities the self is committed to developing. The person whom we admire embodies these personal values and this encourages us to realize our own ideals. The movement of admiration identifies us with the other so that we recognize our own ideal self in the other.

The difference in movement is also reflected in the emotions involving negative recognition. Contempt is directed at an other whom we recognize as not ideal—as the very antithesis of what we want to be. We do not want to recognize our self in the other for whom we feel contempt. In horror, on the other hand, we pull back from an other whom we cannot recognize, an other who is so distorted that we can no longer identify him as a member of our group.

The emotion of horror has been relatively neglected in the psychological literature. However, some of the phenomena that Hebb (1946) has discussed under the rubric of "fear" actually appear to be cases of horror. Hebb's general thesis is that the development of the mammalian brain has gone hand in hand with the development of emotionality and that relatively slight disturbances from ordinary expectancies will provoke fear or, in our terms, horror. The sight of a person with a scarred face may bother us, and even chimpanzees become quite upset when they see a detached model of a chimpanzee head. Hebb argues that the reason we are not aware of the extent of our emotionality is that we carefully control our environment so that deviations will not usually occur. For instance, our taboos with respect to dead bodies and our attempts to isolate the mentally deranged suggest that we are defending ourselves from our own emotional reactions. When these environmental controls break down persons become upset. Holt's (1964) candid description of reactions to a feeble-minded child illustrates this upset, confirming Hebb's speculations and suggesting various methods that we use to distance ourselves from the shock of deviations from "normality."

Our second postulate requires us to find me emotions that

correspond to each of these movements. This leads to some exciting relations and unexpected contrasts. It seems clear that admiration is paired with *pride* and contempt with *shame*. We feel pride when an implicit other admires us and shame when the implicit other feels contempt. This is most apt to occur when the person himself behaves in a way that would evoke his admiration or contempt if some other behaved in that way. That is, he feels pride and displays himself when he does something that he admires; he feels shame and hides himself when he behaves in a way that he finds contemptible.

It is important to note that the implicit other is the person's *own* other rather than some other who may be physically present. Consider the following example. A person who is driving a new foreign car with a stick shift finds that he feels somewhat ashamed when he grinds the car's gears. However, his experience of shame varies with his circumstances, depending on whether a friend is in the car and whether any pedestrians are present. When no one is present, there is no sense of shame; thus, in this particular case, there is no internalized other. When pedestrians are present, the shame is experienced most acutely. However, when a friend is present there is again no shame! To understand these responses we must examine how this person reacts when others grind the gears of their cars. We find that his reaction to others also depends on the circumstances. When he is a pedestrian, he is annoyed by the rasping sound and feels contempt for the "shoddy driving" of the other. However, when he is with a friend who is driving, he blames the "sticky gears" of the car. On the basis of this information we must conclude that when the person himself is driving he sees himself through the eyes of the other who is present, or rather sees himself as he imagines the other sees him. If a friend is present, the person sees himself as innocent, but if a pedestrian is present, the person sees himself through eyes of contempt and feels ashamed.

It should be noted that the person who is experiencing the me emotion of shame, for example, is not consciously aware of an other feeling contempt for him. If the person were, he might respond with an it emotion, such as anger. (In fact, the other is usually experiencing something quite different from what the person imagines.) The person experiencing the me emotion is completely involved in that emotion and consciously experiences the other in whatever way is appropriate. In the case of shame, the person withdraws from the gaze of an other who is experienced as more worthy (rather than as contemptuous). We infer the existence of an implicit other who is contemptuous in order to account for the existence of the shame. The shame itself often seems to function to prevent the contempt of the real other with whom the person is dealing. In fact, in many, and perhaps all, cases the me emotion appears designed to influence the corresponding it emotion of the other—to decrease the probability or intensity of a negative emotion and increase that of a positive emotion.

Let us consider some concrete examples of this from another pair of emotions closely related to the contempt-shame pair—the emotions of disrespect and shyness. A young woman reports feeling shy when she is in the presence of men. On reflection she refines this report and states that she does not feel shy in the presence of all men, but only in the presence of those young men whom she particularly likes. Because shyness is assumed to be paired with disrespect, she is asked what sort of behavior she feels disrespect for. She reports (among other things) feeling disrespect for women who "make a display" of themselves by flirting with men. Now when might we expect this woman to make a display of *herself*? Certainly if she were in the company of a young man to whom she felt attracted. Does she make such a display of herself? Not at all, because she experiences the emotion of shyness and says and does very little. We may thus assume that shyness functions to inhibit the self from the very behavior that the person disrespects in others.

Let us look at another example. A young woman reports feeling shy only when she is in the presence of a particular uncle. She rarely says anything in his presence. She describes him as an extremely intelligent man who regards her highly but does not realize that she is not as bright as he is. At this point in the interview, the experimenter predicts that this subject must disrespect stupidity and that the shyness inhibits her from making remarks that she believes her uncle will consider unintelligent. However, when the subject is asked how she feels about stupid remarks, she replies that she *disapproves* of them. While disapproval is closely related to disrespect, there is a difference which we shall consider in a later chapter. Puzzled, the experimenter asks what would happen if she spoke when her uncle was around. She replies that he would think her remarks stupid, but would attribute them to her not applying herself to her studies. When asked about how she feels about people who do not perform as well as they could because of not trying hard enough, she answers that she disrespects them. We must infer that she assumes that her uncle will also disrespect someone who doesn't really apply herself. In other words, he will disrespect her. Note how this woman takes account of her uncle's thought processes at the same time that she projects her own feelings of disrespect onto her uncle. The resultant feeling of shyness prevents her from talking and forestalls the anticipated disrespect.

Returning to our quest for the me emotions that correspond to the it emotions that deal with recognition, we must ask what emotions correspond to esteem and horror. On the basis of a number of interviews, I believe that esteem may be paired with *humility*, though self-worth might be a better term. By humility I do not, of course, mean a negative feeling of humbleness, but rather a positive regard for the self that is free of arrogance, a naturalness that views the self as simply doing what has to be done, accepts any reward as good fortune rather than something that is due to the self, and helps the self resolve to continue being worthy of any honor it receives. The emotion of humility often occurs when the person is honored by the other and it seems to reinforce this behavior. For example, a young man who is highly regarded by his peers is unable to accompany them on an out-of-state trip because of his lack of money. His friends spontaneously take up a collection for him and present him with the money so that he can go with them. He responds to this demonstration of their esteem with a feeling of humility that enables him to accept their gift with an easy-going appreciation that probably serves to enhance the esteem which they must feel toward him.

The it emotion of horror is, I believe, paired with the me emotion of *guilt*. When a person experiences the emotion of guilt there is an implicit other who is withdrawing in horror from the person. Just as in horror the person cannot recognize the other as the person he once was—cannot identify him as a member of the group—so in guilt the person cannot recognize his self. Paradoxically, this *preserves* the person's identity as a member of the group. Think, for example, of a person who has committed some crime: if he experiences guilt do we not feel less horror than if he experiences nothing?

Consider the following example from an interview in which the respondent was asked to share an experience of guilt. A young woman undergraduate agrees to go to a dance with a man whom she enjoys but does not love. Unexpectedly, a man whom she does love—a boy friend who lives several hundred miles away—comes into town with a surprise present of tickets to a show. But this show is on the night of the other date! She tells her boy friend that she has a previous engagement, but he asks her if she can't break it. After hesitating for a moment, she decides that she will break her date. As soon as this decision is made, she experiences a feeling of guilt. (It has been my repeated experience that guilt and anxiety occur at the point of commitment rather than the point of overt action.) In attempting to determine what the guilt's function is, question after question yields none of the ordinary modes of reducing the guilt. The woman is *not* apparently using the guilt to punish herself. She enjoyed the show and has forgotten about her guilt until the experience is provoked by my initial question. There has been no attempt to confess to the man with whom she broke her engagement. She simply told him her mother was ill but that she would like to see him another time. There is no resolution to "never do such a thing again." In fact, she admits that under like circumstances she probably *shall* do the same thing again. But she still *feels* guilty about it, and even re-experiences some of her guilt as she relates the incident. What "good" is the guilt doing her?

My hypothesis is as follows: This is obviously a nice person and a person who sees herself as a nice person rather than as a "two-timer" who uses men and breaks dates when it happens to be convenient. But, despite the extenuating circumstances, this nice person has, in fact, decided to two-time by breaking a date with a man whom she enjoys in order to go out with her boy friend. Then is she not a two-timer who uses men? No, she is obviously a nice person. But, since she decided to break the date, isn't she a bad person? No, because *she feels guilty* about it. A real two-timer would not feel guilty. Nor is this just a rationalization. Quite the contrary, the guilt *prevents* the kind of rationalization that would make it easier for her to use someone in the future and would turn this woman into a two-timer. The guilt preserves her identity in the face of the fact that she acted wrongly. The guilt says, "In spite of what I did, I do not recognize that as me."

The complete set of recognition emotions, the various pairs, their instructions and transformations are shown in Table 6. It may be noted that each emotion also corresponds to one of the emotions that influence belonging (shown in Table 4). Guilt is the counterpart of anxiety, shame the counterpart of depression, and pride and humility the counterparts of confidence and security respectively.

One of the most interesting features of Table 6 is the fact that it relates emotions which previous investigations have simply contrasted. For example, there have been a number of works that attempt to contrast shame and guilt. Some theorists suggest that shame requires an audience while guilt is internalized; others believe that shame is the effect of a departure from an internalized ego ideal while guilt is a function of the superego, a punishment by an internalized authority whose commands have been transgressed (see Lynd, 1958). If the present analysis is correct, then both shame and guilt are reactions to an implicit other and function to regain his recognition of the self. This other may or may not be internalized. However, in shame the other is contemptuous and does not recognize himself in the person's behavior, whereas in guilt the other is horrified and withdraws recognition of the self as a person or group member.[7]

[7] It has been observed that shame appears to be more of a visual phenomenon (we cower so that the other may not see) whereas guilt is more auditory (the "voice" of authority issues commands). This may have to do with the fact that we experience vision as going out from us (the early theory of vision actually had beams going

TABLE 6
IT AND ME RECOGNITION EMOTIONS

It Emotion	Instruction	Transformation	Me Emotion	Instruction	Transformation
Esteem	Honor other	Other is recognized	Humility	Be worthy	Self is recognized
Admiration	Identify self with other	Ideal self is recognized in other	Pride	Display self	Self is recognized as ideal
Contempt	Dishonor other	Nonideal self is recognized in other	Shame	Hide self	Self is recognized as nonideal
Horror	Disidentify with other	Other is not recognized	Guilt	Atone	Self is not recognized

This analysis does not deny the importance of either ego ideals or the superego. A person's ego ideal is that image by which he hopes to recognize his self. He feels admiration for the other who reflects this ideal, contempt for one who ignores it, and pride or shame when he himself meets or shirks it. Similarly, the demands of authority create the moral imperatives that dictate the behavior by which we recognize a person as a member of the community. We feel esteem for those who follow these values, horror at the spectacle of one who has sinned and thereby cut himself off from the source of all goodness and power, and humility or guilt when we support or oppose these values. However, our analysis suggests that all of these phenomena are related to each other by an underlying matrix — the structure of emotions that make it possible for us to push away, withdraw, extend, or obtain recognition for others and, through them, for ourselves.

BEING

There is a third set of emotions, which may be described in a way that enables us to relate each of the emotions in this set to each other and to corresponding emotions in the sets that govern belonging and recognition. The emotions in this third set govern a relation that may be termed *being*. That is, quite apart from whether or not we belong to or recognize an other, we may grant or deny that the other *is*. Again it might appear at first glance that there is simply a positive or negative possibility here — either the other is or is not. However, for something to *be* for a person, the other must both *exist* (in the sense of being real or alive) and have some meaning, form, or *essence* (the other must exist as something — be it a dog, a cat, a person, or a particular person). Thus a person may not be either by dying or by "not being himself." The different emotions in the set concerned with being operate either by

---

out from the eyes), while we experience audition as coming in toward us. In this respect, shame is related to contempt, which goes out from us in an extension movement (like vision), whereas guilt is related to horror, which involves a contraction in toward the self (like audition).

affecting the other's (or the self's) existence or by affecting the other's (or self's) essence. Let us examine how this is so.

The emotion of *acceptance* confers being on the other by granting the existence of something whose essence seems undesirable. For example, the behavior of an other may seem wrong to us, imperfect in such a fundamental way that we hesitate to grant its existence as a real manifestation of the other. The emotion of acceptance transforms this situation so that we stop insisting that the other meet our own ideal and allow the other a separate be-ing. By accepting the other for what he is, we are confirming his existence—that the way he is now, he is being his essential self rather than "phony" or "wrong." Paradoxically, as Rogers (1961) has emphasized, the moment the other is accepted for himself, he begins to change, usually becoming more like the ideal that was initially demanded. Of course, the "other" may be an unfortunate event rather than a person, a loss or impending loss that one does not want to happen. Here again, the existence of this event may seem basically wrong and unfair—it should not have happened. To accept this event is to let it be—to grant that its existence is essential and has a meaning, a place, even though one does not understand what this meaning is. Then a transformation may occur and the event may be seen from another perspective as something quite different from what was seen before. While we are used to thinking of acceptance as an act rather than as an emotion, this act actually transforms our relationship with the other. And it is not really directly under our control, although we may cultivate it. Hence, from our perspective acceptance may be regarded as an emotion.

In the emotion of *wonder*, we are confronted by the existence of something that we do not understand. The movement of wonder is an attempt to grasp the essence of this miraculous existence—to realize what the other is and thus bring it fully into being. It should be noted that this movement is a contraction, it is toward the self, an attempt to possess meaning, and thus corresponds to the emotions of desire and admiration, while acceptance (like love and esteem) moves toward the being of the other.

The negative counterparts of acceptance and wonder, the

emotions that deny being to the other, are *rejection* and *dread*. In rejection, the imperfect being of the other's existence is denied by making the other meaningless — by denying that there is any essence to the other's existence or any meaning to the occurrence of an event. This emotion has such a powerful effect on the other because we remove his meaning so that he no longer *is* in our eyes. In dread, on the other hand, we understand the essence of the object all too well — its being foretells our own destruction. The movement of the emotion consists of a withdrawal from the possibility of the existence of the other (or event). We hope desperately that it will not come into being.

That me emotions corresponding to each of the emotions that affect the being of the other involve movements that affect the being of the self. In *panic*, for example, Goodman (1975) has shown that the person experiences the self as on the verge of disintegration, as going out of existence. The person desperately tries to hold the self together and keep its being. The self is on the verge of becoming the empty nothingness that we dread. On the other hand, in *serenity* the potential dissolution and loss of the self is welcomed. Rather than feeling nothingness as a vacuum, it is experienced as the no-*thing*-ness that is the source of life — as a plenum, a fullness that is the mother of everything that exists. The dissolution of the self is only apparent, a loss of unessential egoism. In fact, the person's essential self moves toward real existence, just as the other comes into being when he is accepted for what he really is.

The counterpoints to these movements occur in the emotions of *joy* and *sorrow*. In joy, the self is realized or actualized. The person experiences his existence as meaningful, as coming closer to the self that he "really is." While this real self is different from the ideal self that is the concern of the recognition emotions, the being of the real self still has a social component in the sense that an other is implicit. In fact, Lindsay (1975) has shown that when joy occurs, the person experiences the self as "meeting" an other. That is, an other person or object becomes present for the person, acquiring a significance that is filled with meaning in an almost magical way.

In sorrow there is a loss of meaning. A part of the self no longer is and the existence that surrounds us loses its meaning. The emotion demands that we give up our hold on the reality that was, for it is no longer, and unless we surrender our hold we will be living in unreality.

It may be observed that the emotions that govern being are often focused upon by writers concerned with religious issues, and they seem related to what James (1890) termed the "spiritual" self. The entire set with their instructions and transformations are shown in Table 7.

PSYCHOLOGICAL SPACE

Having seen that there are three different sets of eight emotions and that each of the emotions in one set corresponds to a particular emotion in the other sets, we must now inquire as to the relation between these three sets—the relation between belonging, recognizing, and being. We have already seen that these three relations between person and other seem to correspond to the three aspects of the self that James originally described. The material self (one's body, lover, children, home, etc.) may be formed by the belonging emotions, the social self (one's image in the eyes of others) by the recognition emotions, and the spiritual self (one's spirit, soul, mind, psyche) by the emotions concerned with being. In one sense the three different relations may be regarded as three different aspects of the self's identity—what belongs to our self, what is recognized as our self, and what exists as our self. In another sense, the three different relations may be regarded as three different dimensions of the psychological space in which the movements of emotions occur.

Suppose, for example, that the reader is asked which two of the three forms in Figure 10 are closer to each other. In one sense forms 1 and 2 are closer—they are most proximal and belong together; in another sense forms 1 and 3 are closer—

TABLE 7
IT AND ME BEING EMOTIONS

It Emotion	Instruction	Transformation	Me Emotion	Instruction	Transformation
Acceptance	Grant its separate reality	Other gains existence	Serenity	Let it be	Self gains existence
Wonder	Grasp its meaning	Other gains meaning	Joy	Make it real (meet the other)	Self gains meaning
Rejection	Deny its essence	Other's essence is denied, loses meaning	Sorrow	Make it unreal (give up the other)	Self loses meaning
Dread	Deny its reality	Other loses existence	Panic	Do not let it be	Self loses existence

they look more alike and may be recognized as similar; in yet a third sense, forms 2 and 3 are closer—they exist for each other in a unit from which form 1 is excluded. In a crude metaphorical way these three different uses of "closer" correspond to the three different types of psychological distance governed by the three sets of emotions.

This is best understood if we compare the movements of emotions that are identical except for the fact that they occur along different dimensions of psychological space. For example, contrast the emotions of desire, admiration, and wonder. The movements of these emotions are identical in that each involves moving the other closer to the self. However, in desire we wish to possess the other, in admiration we wish to be like the other, and in wonder we wish to understand the other. Now consider the ways in which the other may be pushed away. In anger we remove him, in contempt we make him unlike our self, and in rejection we close the other out of our existence. We may view the three relations as reflecting different aspects of psychological space—they represent three different dimensions along which the other or the self may be moved in order to increase or decrease the distance between the person and the other.

It is interesting to note that the metaphors we use for the various emotions reflect these different dimensions of psycho-

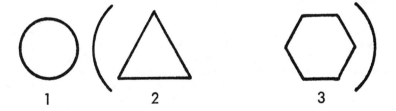

Which two of the three forms are "closer"?

Figure 10. Different Types of Distance

logical space. We speak of the emotions that vary belonging as if they operated on a horizontal plane—pulling an object to us or pushing it away, going toward an object or running away from it. In the recognition dimension we operate in a vertical plane—we "look down on" or "up to" the person for whom we have contempt or admiration. Finally, in dealing with being, we use the metaphors of "in" and "out" as when we are "open" to a person or "close them out."[8] The reader may wish to compare other aspects of these different dimensions by examining the complete matrix of all three sets of emotions shown in Table 8.

THE MATRIX OF EMOTIONS

Table 8 shows that it is possible for us to describe 24 different emotions by conceiving of the particular emotions as movements in a three-dimensional interpersonal space. Any particular emotion is delineated by specifying its position in this matrix of object relations. Any position is specified by four features of the matrix: (1) whether the person or an implicit other is the subject of the movement, (2) whether the movement is toward or away from the other or the person, (3) whether the movement alters the position of the person or the other, and (4) whether the movement occurs along the dimensions of belonging, recognition, or being. How the "choice" of each of these features determines the emotion is illustrated in Figure 11.

It should be noted that some emotions are more alike than

---

[8] The more general problem of distance in interpersonal relations has been intensively explored in a fascinating thesis by Kreilkamp (1970). After a detailed description of 17 different categories of interpersonal distance (such as the distance involved when one person humors another, the distance involved in respect, etc.), he asserts that there are three fundamental distancing processes. These are: the distance involved when a person's behavior is not directed to the person or the other (as in impersonal behavior), the distance involved in failing to be able to take the point of view of the other (as in humoring), and the distance involved in not being in a unit with the other (as in the case of a foreigner). Unfortunately, these types of what might be termed "sociological" distance do not correspond in any simple way with the three types of psychological distance specified above. There is an extremely rich body of material here that cries for investigation.

TABLE 8
THE THREE SETS OF EMOTIONS:
MOVEMENTS ALONG THREE DIMENSIONS OF PSYCHOLOGICAL SPACE

Movement	Dimension		
Toward	Belonging	Recognition	Being
Person moves toward other	Love	Esteem	Acceptance
("Other" moves toward person)	(Security)	(Humility)	(Serenity)
Person moves other toward him	Desire	Admiration	Wonder
("Other" moves person toward him)	(Confidence)	(Pride)	(Joy)
Away			
Person moves other away	Anger	Contempt	Rejection
("Other" moves person away)	(Depression)	(Shame)	(Sorrow)
Person moves away from other	Fear	Horror	Dread
("Other" moves away from person)	(Anxiety)	(Guilt)	(Panic)

others and that their similarity depends on their sharing similar features. Emotions whose movements are similar and that simply differ in the dimension in which the movement occurs are most alike. All the emotions with an implicit other who is the subject of the movement share an intransitive quality since the self is the object of the emotion. And emotions with a toward movement share a positive quality. The emotions where the object's position is altered share a particularly interesting aspect that is not at all self-evident. The relation between the person and the objects of these emotions always entails "oughts" or expectancies, whereas the objects of emotions where the subject's position is altered have an independence from the person that prevents "oughts" or

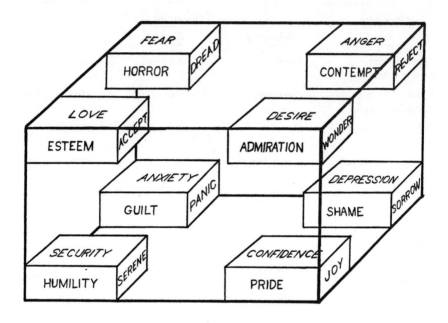

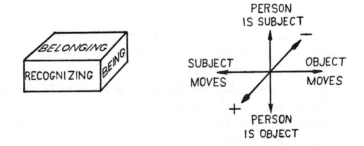

FIGURE 11. Matrix of Emotions

expectancies from operating. In the next chapter we shall see that the person who is angry believes the other ought to have behaved differently whereas he does not feel this way about a feared object. Similarly, while possession of the other—the aim of desire—entails expectancies and the fact that the other ought to behave in certain ways, such oughts are antithetical to love, which requires that the other have freedom.

Another aspect of the matrix which is of possible theoretical importance is the implication that it may be easier to move from one emotion to another when only one feature is changed. For example, it has often been observed that the emotional state of a person who is depressed may alter so that the person feels either anger or extreme confidence. The matrix suggests that anxiety may also be a possible alternative state, whereas security and fear are less likely since they involve a change of two features and love is least likely as an alternative since it involves a shift of three features. However, this suggestion must be qualified as it may be much easier to reverse certain features than others.

THE CONCEPT OF CHOICE

The idea of a matrix of the emotions suggests that any particular emotion is the outcome of a pattern of "choices" that organize our relationship with the other. This may be best understood if we compare such a model to the perceptual model suggested by the transactional school of Ames (1951) and his associates.

The transactional school holds that any perception is really an interpretation of a situation and, hence, involves implicit choices. For example, suppose that a circle of light is reflected onto the retina of one eye of a seated subject. If the circle grows bigger the structure of the situation permits only two interpretations. The subject may see the circle either as growing bigger or as moving toward him. Since both views are consistent with the pattern of illumination on the retina, there is an ambiguity in the situation and the subject must "choose" what to see. However, unlike the conscious decisions we are accustomed to making, the subject is not aware that he has a decision to make, he is unaware that there are two alternatives. It may be objected that under such circumstances the subject does not really make a decision. But there is clearly a choice involved rather than a mechanical reaction. I shall therefore call such an event a "choice" (using the term in a technical sense and reserving the term "decision" for conscious choices).

The Ames's demonstrations clearly reveal these choices. For example, if a subject looks with one eye into a tunnel while the experimenter inflates a round balloon at the other end, the subject will tend to see a ball moving toward him. This is how he chooses to interpret the growing image on his retina (Hastorf, 1950). Note that this perception is not a construction built out of the air. It is a choice based on an existential structure, the sphere *must* be either moving toward him *or* getting bigger. It cannot, for example, be moving away.[9] Which of the possible choices is made may depend on past experience and other situational considerations.

It is also important to note that a subject will continue to make this choice even though *intellectually* he knows that his perception is in error. For example, he will see an approaching ball even though he knows that a stationary balloon is being inflated—even if he sees the apparatus with his own eyes. The *perception* will only change—he will only make the correct choice—when he *acts* at the same time he is choosing. For example, he may try to touch the sphere that appears to be moving toward him. Only then will the perception suddenly pop and the subject perceive a stationary ball that is growing larger.

Emotion shares many characteristics with perception. While both seem to be passive, we know perception is behavior and we may surmise that every time a person has an emotion there are, in fact, choices of which the person is not aware. And, as we all know, an intellectual knowledge of our situa-

---

[9] The other possible alternatives—that the subject is moving closer or is growing smaller—are ruled out by the absence of the other stimuli that would occur if either of these were happening.

tion does not suffice to let us choose differently. In such cir-cumstances, only action — and action that may seem inappro-priate — will enable us to have the emotion that is veridical and called for by the actual situation we are in.

Let us consider the structure of choices that may underlie an emotion. Rather than a circle of light on the retina, we have a situation where some event has occurred that involves the person's self, an event that "moves" him. However, there are different ways that a person can organize what has happened, different choices he can make that will yield quite different interpretations of his situation and transform his way of being-in-the-world. The choices he makes organize an emotional structure that transforms his situation and instructs (or demands) him to behave in specified ways.

These choices as to how to interpret his situation and organize his life space are the features specified above. That is, the person must choose whether the distance between himself and the other should decrease or increase and along what dimension of psychological space, whether he or the other should be the subject of movement, and whether his own or the object's position must be altered. Of course there are times when a given choice is highly unlikely. Confronted with an other who pulls a knife there is some choice about whose position will be altered but little likelihood that a movement will be made toward rather than away from the other.

On the other hand, there is always the possibility of a re-versal of choices that completely alters the structure of the emotional situation. When a person's mood changes, when there is progress in therapy, or when there is a religious con-version, we often encounter emotions that demonstrate an un-usual interpretation of events. There are hundreds of accounts of such dramatic changes. For example, *Guideposts* (Eller-busch, 1976) reports the story of a man whose five-year-old child was run down and killed while dutifully crossing the street at the school crossing. The father was thrown into a depression that was mixed with grief ("If such a child can die — then life is meaningless and faith in God is self-delu-sion"). The following morning the police found the hit-and-run driver — a juvenile from a broken home who had stolen his mother's car. The father's emotion then changed to hatred ("Get him tried as an adult"). Late that night the father, pacing the hall, reports praying—"show me why!"—and suddenly experiencing a Person who filled the hall with love ("It was like a lightning stroke that turned out to be the dawn"). His own emotions were transformed into love and joy. Convinced of purpose in the universe, he asks for the release of the juvenile and his house becomes the boy's second home.

Since whatever emotion is experienced is the product of a number of unconscious choices, there are many more degrees of freedom in a person's life than are usually recognized. However, once these choices are made, there are inevitable consequences; the emotional organization requires definite perceptions and inter- and intrapersonal relationships. These consequences are analogous to the requirements of geometry. Given the task of drawing a line through a circle, we may choose to have the line pass through one point or two. However, if it passes through one point it must necessarily be at right angles to the radius at that point. To better understand the nature of the choices underlying any given emotion and the necessary consequences that follow we must examine the particular emotions in more detail. Therefore in the next chapter we shall leave the over-all matrix of emotions and examine the individual structure of a particular emotion. In Chapter Four we shall return to the general matrix in order to consider whether there are still other choices and sets of emotions that must be described.

Chapter Three

THE ANALYSIS OF AN EMOTION

From the perspective of a structural theory, we may analyze any emotion by articulating a structure that is peculiar to the particular emotion and yet will enable us to relate it to an over-all structure—a network of relations among all the emotions. The method of analysis—our procedure of investigation—can, in principle, be applied to any emotion. Let us consider the emotion of anger.

It is possible to ask two quite different questions about the experience of anger. First, taking the idea of anger for granted, we may ask about the different ways in which anger is experienced. The pursuit of this question begins to reveal the full scope of meanings that anger has for different persons, in different cultures, at different stages of development, and in different instances in the circumstances of a person's life. Asking such a question leads us to discover that individuals may experience anger quite differently. Some are overwhelmed by the intensity of their anger and tend to avoid the experience; others view anger as a necessary evil—an unpleasant experience that is sometimes demanded by their circumstances. Still others enjoy feeling the flow of anger and find that this helps them to define their self. Some cultures view anger indulgently, others (such as our own) are ambivalent, and others (such as the Utku eskimoes) view anger as a decidedly inferior way of being which is indulged in only by children, whites, and others without the full use of their reason (Briggs, 1970). In the infant, anger has an undirected quality that may be expressed in a clenching of the fists, a flushing of the skin, an arching of the back with vigorous kicking of the limbs and constant yowling. By age six there is an "other" at whom one is angry, who ought to have behaved differently, and whom one wishes to hurt. The adult may feel the same desire yet mask his anger completely. Within the same person, anger may be expressed in different forms. This is demonstrated by Deming's (1971) differentiation between the murderous anger that a person may feel when his existence is threatened and the anger, born of hope for change, that assertively demands an end to an injustice. One may also ask about the development or formation of an individual instance of anger and note whether it grows out of a situation of frustration, a feeling of being unloved, or a sudden confrontation with another's will. An outburst of anger may simply mean that a person is frustrated, or it may mean that the person is feeling unloved and needs reassurance, or that he is seriously demanding a change in another's behavior. All these meanings of anger (as well as the various clinical questions raised by Schafer [1964] and summarized in the first chapter) are aspects of the answer to our first question as to how anger is experienced.

But I now want to focus on quite a different question. Our first question takes the essence of anger for granted and asks about the different ways in which it exists. The second question addresses the existence of this essence. It asks: *what* is anger? How, for example, does it differ from fear? Given the many different manifestations of anger, what makes us recognize them all as *anger*? What makes us experience anger as anger rather than as fear, contempt, or depression? What is *essential* to the meaning of anger no matter how its existence is manifested?

Of course, to ask such a question makes the assumption that there *is* something essential to the experience of anger. It assumes that the emotion that is overpowering to one person and pleasurable to another, that is valued by one culture and prohibited by another, that is expressed in different ways as a person develops, that may lead to murder or appropriate assertion is in some sense the same emotion. That is, in fact, implied when we use one term — "anger" — or speak of the "different experiences of anger" as though anger were something that might be expressed in different experiences. In Lewin's

(1935) terminology, our search for the essence of anger is a search for a "genotypic" form, a form that is manifested in phenotypes that depend on the particular circumstances of the life space.

In searching for what is essential to the experience of anger, we are involved in constructing a meaning for anger that will fit all experiences of anger and distinguish them from other experiences. Ideally, such a construction can be related to essential statements about other psychological events (such as fear, contempt, and depression) and this is precisely what a structural theory attempts to accomplish. To achieve such a conceptualization we shall use a method of inquiry that I call "conceptual encounter" because it involves an encounter between the conceptualization of what is essential to anger (or whatever other idea is the focus of concern) and the actual existence of concrete instances of the phenomena. In the course of this encounter, the existence of concrete instances of anger may change one's conceptualization of what the essence of anger is. On the other hand, the existence of a good conceptualization may change how a person experiences concrete instances of the phenomenon. Thus, a dialectical process is involved in the encounter.

There are four criteria by which a conceptualization may be judged. First, the essential structure should apply to every concrete instance of anger that exists or can be imagined to exist. Second, the conceptualization should be precise enough to distinguish instances of the phenomena from the existence of other phenomena (such as fear or contempt). Third, the conceptualization should be insightful enough to reveal or make explicit what was before only implicit in the phenomena, so that we are now aware of new features of the phenomena and see it in a different light and perhaps in places where we had not noticed it before. Fourth, the conceptualization should relate to other abstractions—other constructions of essential structures—in a parsimonious way that reveals the interconnections between different phenomena. An answer to the question, "What is essential to anger?", should apply to all instances of anger, should distinguish them from instances of other emotions, should give us insight into and appreciation for the richness of the phenomena of anger, and should enable us to see how it relates to other phenomena.[1]

THE SITUATION IN WHICH ANGER ARISES

If we consider the experience of anger and contrast it with the experience of fear, it becomes apparent that whenever we are angry we somehow believe that we can influence the object of our anger. We assume that the other is responsible for his actions and ought to behave differently. He "should not" behave as he is behaving. On the other hand, when we fear someone there is no question of what the other "should" do. In a sense, the other is alien to us and we feel we have no rights to communicate. The analysis of numerous experiences of anger suggests that the relation between the angry person and the object of his anger always has this interesting aspect of community—that the other should somehow behave in an expected way. The other's behavior constitutes a challenge to what the person believes ought to exist. In light of this, I shall advance the following conceptualization: If, in a person (p)'s experience, an other (o) *challenges* what p *asserts ought* to exist, then p will be angry at o. Conversely, if p is angry at o, then in p's experience o is challenging what p asserts ought to exist.

Each of the concepts in a statement such as the one above has implications that can be specified so that the relations between all of the concepts and the phenomena become clear. In the above statement there are three key concepts: ought, challenge, and assertion. We shall deal with each of them in order.

The concept of *ought* has been analyzed by Heider (1958). The concept implies a force on behavior coming from a "suprapersonal objective order." What *ought* to exist is not simply what an individual *wants* to exist but is equivalent to

---

[1] Such an enterprise is an aspect of phenomenology and entails the careful examination of experience, the technique of imaginative variation and, in my own method, the contrasting of different experiences in order to gain insight into the essential structure of a phenomenon.

what an accepted objective order wants to exist. The concept is related to the concept of *value* in that if an individual has a value, he believes that the objective order is so constituted that *under certain conditions* persons *ought* to behave in certain ways. The concept of ought is also related to the concept of *can* in that we would not say that a person ought to do something if it is clearly impossible for him to do this. If p ought to do x it is implied that p *can* do x—that p is a possible cause of x.

Heider also points out that since oughts are perceived as coming from an objective order they (and values) have the same status as a belief in what is real. Whereas another person may have likes and wants that are quite different from our own, if he has values or oughts that are different it is as upsetting as if he saw red where we see green. The mere fact of a value disagreement creates tension in an interpersonal relationship.

There are a number of other tensions connected with values and oughts which Heider has explicated. Often the mere fact that something exists suggests that it ought to exist, and we sometimes act as though what ought to exist actually did exist. We feel that a person who does what he ought to do, *ought* to be happy, and the mere fact that somebody is unlucky is sometimes enough to convince us that he has done something he ought not to have done. While these pressures clearly exist it is not evident why they should exist. Recently Lerner (1974) has suggested that the relations stem from basic contracts which the person makes as he becomes socialized.

We may extend the analysis of ought by noting three important facts. First, oughts do not apply to everything or everybody but only to members of one's community. Most persons do not feel a dog ought to be charitable with his bones and many persons do not feel a foreigner ought to be patriotic or respect the dead. To the extent that we do feel strangers ought to do certain things we are including them in a broad community of humans to which we see ourselves as belonging.

Second, each person has the choice of whether or not to join a community, whether or not to belong. Fingarette (1967) points out that one cannot force a person to be "responsible" (to obey oughts) and that many persons living in our society (e.g., psychopaths) have never really decided to be responsible — to join a community. While we may act as if another person belongs and while our emotions are governed by our determination of whether or not the other belongs, in fact, only that person can decide whether or not he belongs.

Third, although up to now our analysis has been in terms of fairly universal values and oughts, the concept may also be applied to smaller communities which may, in fact, only contain two persons (e.g., a husband and wife). For instance, property rights with their related set of oughts and duties only apply within a national community, membership in a private club may require the acceptance of a specific set of oughts pertinent only to club members, and the rights of a husband or of a wife (or any couple "committed" to each other) include the right to expect a response to personal needs and, hence, involve values and oughts that only pertain to that particular couple. I shall call any group whose members recognize a common set of values, a unit. A unit may be as small as two persons or as large as the community of humans, but in every case persons decide whether or not to belong to it, and if they accept the responsibility of belonging they become subject to and may take advantage of the values held by members of the unit.

Given the above conceptualization of ought, we may now see how this concept relates to various emotions. Since anger is the assertion of an ought, the angry person must perceive the other person to have the same values and, hence, to be in a unit with him — to belong to a unit with a set of expectancies. Similarly, the angry person must perceive the other to be responsible for his actions and, hence, capable of behaving differently.

It should be noted that we are speaking here of the subjective experience at the moment of anger rather than of what may be objectively true. Obviously there are occasions when a person gets angry at a small child who cannot really help his behavior or explodes at a stuck door that is not really subject to the oughts of any of the units to which he belongs. However, *at the moment* of anger the child *is* held responsible (no matter how sorry one may feel later), and the door *ought* to open (though one knows intellectually that doors are not human). Adults are somewhat removed from the obvious magical thinking involved in such cases, but children may be quite aware that they are distorting reality. I recently witnessed the angry explosion of a seven-year-old girl at a sled, which kept falling down no matter how it was propped up against a wall. Talking with her afterward I asked why she was angry and she patiently explained that the "darned old thing" wouldn't stay up. As she was talking a grin flitted across her face. I asked her why she had smiled and (after some "do tell me's") she stated, "Well, I *told* it to stay up — I know it can't really *do* things, but I haven't had a thing I wanted all day long, so I told it to and it should have" — and here she smiled again. One only wishes that most adults were as much in touch with their infantile behavior.

The most primitive expression of anger appears to be the rage that an infant demonstrates when it is subjected to pain. From our perspective this rage, which is reflected in vasodilation, extension of the limbs, and yowling, is a removal of the pain — a thrusting away of something that the infant "decides" ought not to be. While obviously an infant does not have the complex network of social oughts that later develops, I believe that we are dealing here with a genuine ought and not simply a wish. The infant's *will* is clearly manifest and I suspect that this insistence — that the pain shall not be — is the root source of morality.

The fact that anger involves another member of one's unit and the application of ought forces is in sharp contrast to the phenomenon of fear. The concept of fear implies that the other person or object does *not* belong to any of one's operative units. There can be no communication in fear because there are no common values that the other is violating; the other appears as a member of a different species. Theorists have sometimes attempted to distinguish anger from fear on the basis of relative power, but a child may get quite angry at an obviously stronger adult and an adult may be afraid of a child (e.g., if the child might misbehave in front of an important visitor). The essential difference appears to lie in the fact that common values are at issue in anger but not in fear.

While fear is related to seeing the *other* as not belonging to the unit, we may regard anxiety as related to seeing one*self* as not belonging to the unit. If, for example, one takes responsibility for violating an ought force one begins to no longer belong to the unit because one has repudiated the values of the unit and separation occurs.

The concept of *challenge* is also implicit in the concept of anger. Anger implies that the other should change his behavior and act as a responsible member of the person's unit. But a mere request, reminder, or command might accomplish this. The presence of anger indicates that a *challenge* must be present. The other is seriously acting as though what *he* thinks ought to exist is reality, and this differs from what the person asserts ought to exist. Since, as we have noted, only one of these oughts can be correct, there is a real conflict of wills where one may win or lose; the contenders occupy the same "reality space" and one must leave.

Since the concept of challenge implies that the other is a serious contender for the space, an alternative to anger is to perceive the other in such a way that he is not a real contender. This may be done in a number of different ways: (1) The other may be perceived as not responsible for his action, i.e., drunk, insane, only a child. Because the other cannot really control his behavior, the ought does not apply to him. (2) The other may be regarded as unqualified to be a challenger because of his status, i.e., a foreigner, a woman, a member of a different caste. The other does not challenge the ought because it does not apply to him. (3) The other may be seen as having a character structure that works against his being an adequate member of the group, i.e., he is perceived as phony, disagreeable, basically weak. In this case, the other is usually disliked, and this sentiment takes the place of anger.

Note that all these ways of perceiving the other involve increasing the *distance* between oneself and the other. Rather than getting angry, the other is seen as different from oneself so that he cannot present a real challenge. Instead of the emotional force of anger, we have a structural change—in effect, a change in psychological space so that a person who may have been close is now distant. Often this increase in distance is accompanied by rejection or contempt and the emotion of anger would be preferable. However, an increase in distance is not necessarily a negative act. It may, for example, involve a separation of the person from an object to which he was fused and the acceptance of genuine differences.

The concept of *assertion* is also necessarily implied by the concept of anger. While anger implies that both the angry person and the other belong to an identical unit and thus recognize the same values, these two persons do not necessarily agree on what ought to exist. Just as liking only becomes wanting when a person also has a need, values become oughts only when a person also recognizes that certain conditions exist. One may value truth yet not experience an ought to tell the truth when a person who is on his or her way to a dance asks about an unbecoming outfit. The situation that is perceived to exist requires reassurance rather than frankness. In most contests there is a disagreement over what actually exists (including, of course, the meaning of what exists). The contest is over what reality is like and, hence, what ought to be done. For one person the salient features of the situation indicate that x ought to be done; for the other person the situation calls for y. The concept of anger implies that in this contest the person continues to assert his position (what he personally recognizes as existent) and what oughts apply. Without anger, the person may "fold" and give in to the other's position.

If the person chooses to blame himself rather than the other, if he holds himself responsible for violating the values of the unit so that he is the one who ought to behave differently, then the other becomes the subject for the movement and the person experiences the emotion of depression rather than anger. Depression is therefore an alternative to anger, and one that is quite different from the various ways of distancing oneself from the other. In fact, depression probably occurs when values are being challenged but anger seems unprofitable and there are reasons (such as dependency) against exercising alternatives that create distance. In this sense, depression, like anger, serves to preserve closeness. However, as an antithesis to anger, depression robs a person of his will and thus prevents him from acting on the basis of his values. Such a response may be quite functional in that the actions required by the person's values might have destructive consequences.

In the case of a direct conflict with another, the person may see that the other is stronger and that he must relinquish his claim and acknowledge the other's version of reality. Here depression may be related to the surrender mechanisms that the members of some species utilize as a signal that they are defeated. Such signals end the fight and prevent harm to the loser (the victor being compelled to inhibit further aggressive action) (Lorenz, 1952). Kane (1976) has suggested that in all cases of situational depression the depressed person is caught in a situation where his values require an action that would have destructive consequences. The depression occurs to prevent the required action, thus preventing the consequences while still preserving the person's commitment to his values and, hence, his group membership.

As one of several examples, Kane cites the case of a teenager who, believing that premarital sex is permissible and that contraceptives work, becomes pregnant. Her value that human life is sacred calls for her to have the child. However, her young boy friend is not in a position to marry her and she feels she cannot depend on, or even confide in, her mother, who is opposed to premarital sex. While there was some anger at the mother (who "ought to accept sex"), the predominant emotion in this case was a mild depression which lasted for about a month as the young woman decided she *had* to have an abortion. Note how the depression structures the situation so that she cannot *act* (i.e., she *has* to have the abortion). In this way, she experiences no guilt and her values are maintained in spite of the fact that she does not behave in accord with them.

If this structural analysis is correct, depression occurs when a person must both preserve his values (and, hence, the closeness of the unit of which he is a member), yet must not act in the way that he believes these values require. The emotion of depression solves this conflict by making the person unable to act in the way his values require. This preserves the values of the unit in that the person is not acting and his behavior thus does not challenge its values. Consequently, there is no threat of losing unit membership and no anxiety. However, such a solution necessarily entails a loss of position—the person is "no good" in that he cannot uphold the values of the group and, hence, is not wanted by the other.

In contrast to the emotion of depression, where the person holds the self responsible in the sense that he ought to have acted differently (the implicit other removing the self), anger always involves the assertion that the *other* is responsible and ought to behave differently. This assertion of the person's own position as to what ought to exist—a manifestation of his will—is an intrinsic aspect of the situation in which anger occurs.

The concept of a *situation* in which anger occurs requires a number of qualifications. First, the situation, in this case one in which the person experiences a challenge to what he asserts ought to exist, is not independent of the person, but rather is constituted by the person's choices. The emotional meaning of an event and the entire situation in which a person finds himself are dependent on these choices. The person may choose to experience the other as in a unit with similar values or as an alien; he may experience a challenge or create distance, assert that he is right and the other ought to behave differently or feel that his own self ought to be different. Of course, these choices are not conscious and are often over-determined by information about the other but, in principle, different choices could be made and the person has the potential freedom to give the situation a different meaning.

On the other hand, every choice has implicit consequences that necessarily follow from how the situation is structured. For instance, if the other is perceived to be behaving in a way that violates the person's values, then the person *must* respond in certain ways. He may become angry or he may increase the distance between himself and the other, but he cannot remain close without becoming angry. Rather than choose one of these alternatives, he may perceive a conflict but choose to see himself as violating what ought to be. However, then he must become depressed. There are still other alternatives. For example, I have not discussed the possibility of feeling hurt, or of allowing the pain of separation. But I believe the central point is clear: psychological reality is structured in such a way that any choice we make affects the entire system of intra- and interpersonal relations in specifiable ways. The task of a structural psychology is to explicate this network of relations.

Finally, we cannot really separate the person's perception of his situation from his response to this situation. In a sense his response is precisely what structures his situation. We state that if a person perceives a challenge to what he asserts ought to exist, then he will become angry. However, we also state that a person who is angry is engaged in the act of removing a challenge to what he asserts ought to exist. Thus, the act of anger is not really a response to a situation as much as a way of structuring a situation, a way of organizing the relation between the person and the environment. The person is in a transaction with the environment, his angry will—his assertion of his view of what ought to exist—is an aspect of the very situation his anger responds to.

THE EXPRESSIVE TRANSFORMATIONS OF ANGER

Spinoza once defined emotions as ". . . the modifications of the body, whereby the active power of the said body is increased or diminished, ordered or constrained, and also the ideas of such modifications" (1675, p. 130). From our perspective, every emotion is expressed in transformations of the body and/or the body's relation to its environment. In the case of anger there is often extensive involvement of skeletal muscles—the person stiffens his muscles, clenches his fists, frowns, etc. Ax's (1960) investigation suggests that when anger is contrasted with fear, there is more apt to be a decrease in heart rate and an increase in diastolic blood pressure, muscle tension, and number of galvanic skin responses when the person is angry. Since this pattern of responses is only true on the average and accounts for only about a third of the variance of the measures, it seems probable that anger has substantially different physiological effects in different persons and in different situations. However, as our understanding of the emotion increases it may be possible to discover some bodily manifestations that are equivalent in all instances of anger.

It is interesting to note that the expressive transformation of an emotion is *not* identical with the affective bodily responses for which we have names, such as laughing, crying, blushing, yawning. In fact, Funk's (1974) study of laughter suggests that each of these "body affects" has a structure of its own and occurs when emotion is not a possible solution for the situation in which we find ourselves. Laughter occurs when there is a paradox in how we experience reality, a paradox that cannot be solved without losing the gravity of reality and levitating into a region of low gravity as our body oscillates with laughter. Such laughter is quite different from the laughter that may be an expressive part of joy or the hollow laugh of despair.

In the case of anger, the most evident effect on the body is not any particular physiological response, but rather an apparent increase in volitional capacity.[2] If we conceive of anger as a force that preserves the reality the person asserts against the force generated by the other's challenge, we may view this force as functioning to strengthen the person's will so that he continues to assert his position and to act in accord with the way in which he perceives reality and with the rights that he claims. My own experience and the results of a number of interviews seem to indicate that anger is sometimes necessary for the maintenance of will in the face of the opposition's position and possible use of retaliation. If the anger is unavailable, or insufficient, the person folds and fails to assert himself.

The volitional effect of anger is illustrated in the following examples. The first two reveal the unfortunate consequences of *not* getting angry. A young faculty member of a small liberal arts college joins a number of students on a peace march in Washington to protest the war in Vietnam. The next

[2] Cannon (1915) refers to F. Russell (1904-1905, p. 243) who "relates a tale told by the Indians to their children, in which an enraged coyote was chasing some quails. 'Finally the quails got tired,' according to the story, 'but the coyote did not, for he was angry and did not feel fatigue.' "

day he is eating with a small faculty group at a table in the college dining hall. The colonel of the college's ROTC unit, who is at the table, states, "If we had a better sports program here these students wouldn't disgrace themselves by going off on these foolish marches." The young faculty member remains silent, but later reports that he wishes he had said something. He feels he has "sold out." It is my conjecture that more is involved here than a fear that the colonel will consider the young man to be a fool and a disgrace to the college. If this were the fear, and if the colonel's opinion were politically important, the younger man would simply feel angry and make a rational decision to assert himself in a different way at a different time and place. This would not be a sell-out of his own position. We surmise that, in fact, the younger man has some doubts about his position and feels that he may lose in a public contest and thereby *actually become* a foolish disgrace. To protect his self-image as an intelligent credit to the college, he has to remain quiet. However, in doing this, he abandons the field of social reality to the colonel. In fact, if he asserted himself by saying something like, "I beg your pardon, Colonel, but I participated in that march myself and felt it was my duty as a citizen," the colonel might apologize or fall silent. In either case the younger man would establish his position in a social reality—that to participate in a peace march is a responsible thing to do. In reality it would be difficult for the colonel to publicly maintain his position that the march was foolish, and almost impossible for him to completely win the field by asserting that the younger man had proved himself to be a foolish disgrace to the college. By using distance—"what can you expect from a ROTC colonel"—in order to avoid anger, the younger faculty member is left without the strength to assert his own will and the colonel wins the contest.

A student writes a paper for a course and believes that she has done a good job. It is returned with a mark of D+. She later reports that rather than becoming angry she had two thoughts in quick succession: "He [the grader] obviously doesn't know what I am talking about" and, "The course has a pass-fail option anyway, so nuts with grades." In the first thought distance is created by considering the reader as unintelligent, whereas in the second thought the student sees herself as uncommitted to the course and abandons the claim to a good grade. Note that without anger the student is unable to maintain the assertion that she ought to get the grade her paper deserves. Again, we conjecture that she is unwilling to risk an actual confrontation with the reader about the grade for fear that she shall lose and her paper will *really* be worth only a D+.

A woman in public relations work is given a contract to change the image of a firm which is expanding its business. After doing some work on the contract she has lunch with a member of the firm and happens to express her political views. She notices that the conversation grows strained and realizes that she has made a mistake in speaking so openly about her beliefs. The job calls for further contracts with the firm but her client does not call and cannot be reached. This places the woman in conflict. On the one hand, a contract has been signed, some work has been done, and she should attempt to collect her fee. On the other hand, her client is in a position where he may injure her reputation with other clients if he promulgates his judgment of her. Consequently she hesitates to press him for payment. She later reports that she would not have taken legal steps to collect the fee if she were not so angry about the client condemning her professional ability because of her politics, and about his failing to cancel the contract in a responsible way. Because of her anger she has her lawyer write a letter threatening court action and thereby collects half of the fee called for by the contract.

To summarize: while the bodily effects of anger may differ from person to person, the emotion always seems related to an increase in the person's power of assertion just as depression seems tied to a decrease in that power. My own conjecture is that the volitional effects of emotions are closely related to the bodily manifestations.

THE INSTRUCTIONAL TRANSFORMATION OF ANGER

We have seen that anger may be regarded as an instruction to the person to remove the challenge to his values posed by the other's behavior. Sometimes this removal is fantasied as a destruction of the other—a desire to tear him apart—or it is acted out in verbal or physical blows, but it may also be accomplished by a straightforward assertion that operates to affect the other directly. We have noted that distance may be substituted for anger and the other viewed as not responsible for his actions. On the other hand, if anger occurs there is a definite implication that the other is responsible as a member of the unit and that one holds him responsible and demands a change in his behavior. The effect of anger depends on its appropriateness and the state of the other person. The other may have been trying to get away with something (either consciously or in unconscious "bad faith"). If so, he may have been distorting reality to fit his personal convenience, or he may have been taking advantage of the rights associated with belonging to a unit, without really belonging (that is, accepting the responsibility of obeying the oughts of the membership). In such cases, anger will often operate to pull the other up short and end his game playing. The anger may also operate to make the other aware that he *is* a member of a unit in spite of the fact that he had never realized this before. If the person is not open to the anger and a defense is utilized, then he will distort himself or reality in some way and it may be necessary for the angry person to recognize this and no longer hold the person directly responsible for his behavior. Accordingly, he is free to circumvent the other's position and to avoid giving him real responsibility or rights in the area in question. Ideally, however, the anger operates so that the other person begins to act as a responsible member of the group.

The interpersonal benefits of anger—as operating to hold another responsible—are illustrated by an account in Hannah Green's (1964) *I Never Promised You a Rose Garden*. The patients on a mental hospital ward have been unmercifully badgering a new attendant (Ellis) who they sense is close to being crazy himself. They compare him to an attendant (Hobbs) who has recently committed suicide. After narrowly averting an explosion of hatred on the ward, an attendant who is liked (McPherson) stops by the main character's (Deborah) bed:

"Deb," he said gently, "lay off on Mr. Ellis, will you?"

"Why me?" she said.

"I want all of you to let him alone. No more jokes. No more references to Hobbs."

"Are you going to tell everybody?" (The guarded vying-for-favor and the guarded suspicion of all the world's motives and representatives overcame prudence and forced the question.)

"Yup," he said. "Everybody on the ward."

"Even Marie and Lena?" (They were acknowledged to be the sickest on the ward, even by the patients.)

"Deb . . . just lay off."

For a moment she felt that he was using her. He was the only one who could get away with calling the patients by nicknames without sounding strained, but it sounded strained now.

"Why me? I thought you normal ones had agreed that we were out of it—your conventions and routines. I'm not nice and I'm not polite and I know more about Hobbs than you do. He was one of *us!* The only thing that separated him from us was three inches of metal key he used to fondle for assurance. Ellis is another one. I know about him and his hate."

McPherson's voice was low, but his anger was real, and Deborah felt it coming from a place in him that he had never shown before.

"Do you think the sick people are all in hospitals? Do you girls think you have a corner on suffering? I don't want to bring up the money business—it's been overdone—but I want to tell you right now that lots of people on the outside world would *like* to get help and can't. You ought to know mental trouble when you see it. You don't bait other patients. I've never heard you say anything against one of them." (She remembered what she had said to Carla and the stroke of guilt felt again for it.) "Lay off Ellis, Deb—you'll be glad for it later."

"I'll try."

He looked down hard at her. She could not see his face in the shadow, but she sensed that it was in repose. Then he turned and walked out of the dormitory. Deborah fought the sedative for a while thinking about what he had said and how. It was tough but true, and under the anger of it ran the tone—the tone rare anywhere, but in a mental ward like a priceless jewel—the tone of a simple respect between equals. The terror she felt at the responsibility it bore was mingled with a new feeling. It was joy [pp. 93-94].*

There are a number of points which should be observed in the above example. First, note that the example fits our description of the conditions for anger. McPherson acts assertively on the basis of the way he believes things ought to be. He tells Deborah (a human being) to stop hurting another human being. Deborah challenges this assertion—in effect, saying that it's not her problem because she is in a different unit from "you normal ones". She asserts that Ellis, though he masquerades as a guard and holds the keys, really has no human rights because he is sick.

Second, McPherson's anger is directed at an inconsistency in Deborah's arguments. He *agrees* with her that Ellis is sick and then points out to her that she doesn't hurt other sick people. In effect, McPherson insists that Deborah is in the same unit of humanity that he is, and that she is not really acting on the basis of conviction that Ellis is sick. Deborah's challenge is based on her own uncertainty that she is as good as Ellis is and her own related self-hate.

Third, the anger is "clean" and operates directly on Deborah without the use of any threats. McPherson does not downrate Deborah; he angrily asserts his position. He is *open*—the anger "coming from a place in him he had never shown before." And, in a sense, he is vulnerable. By getting angry, he has given up control, and would be hurt if Deborah responded with hate.

Fourth, the anger operates directly to change Deborah's behavior. McPherson's assumption that she is a fellow human being with rights and responsibilities makes Deborah realize that she *is* a human being and she accepts those responsibilities.

Fifth, McPherson *has* to get angry if he is not to increase distance—view Deborah as basically not responsible—and thereby distort her reality and make himself inauthentic. In this case, getting angry—and at a mental patient— is extremely functional.

I am not arguing that the expression of anger is always beneficial. The anger itself may be inappropriate—based on a false perception of the situation or used as a pretense that is functioning to avoid anxiety. Or the anger may be appropriate but misused in an attempt to destroy or dominate the other. This often occurs when a person feels threatened by the challenge posed by the other or when the person is unable to risk or is unacquainted with the value of simply openly expressing the anger. But when anger is both appropriate and openly expressed, it functions to help the other take responsibility and thus maintains the values of the unit.

In one sense the instructional transformation appears to always be successful. The act of anger—the imperative "this must stop"—psychologically removes the challenge so that the person is convinced of his own position as to what ought to exist, regardless of whether or not the other's behavior is changed.

THE FUNCTION OF ANGER

Chein (1972) indicates that all of a person's behavior may be regarded as activity that is both directed toward objects and included in other behavior. For example, the behavior of reading this sentence is an activity of the reader that is both directed toward an object (the sentence) and included in other behavior (the activity of reading this monograph and the activity of gaining a better understanding of the emotions). From this perspective, all behavior is motivated by the behaviors in which it is included and a motive is simply a behavior that includes other behaviors (e.g., comprehending emotions is a motive for reading this sentence).

We have seen that the emotion of anger is an activity that is directed toward the removal of a challenge to what the person asserts ought to exist. This activity—this whole way of organizing the person's relationship with the other—functions to preserve the person's position as to what ought to exist, to preserve the values that these oughts reflect, and to preserve the closeness inherent in perceiving the other as a member of one's unit. It is included in these other activities which, in turn, are included in the vast network of the person's many ongoing concerns. In this respect, anger and all other emotions are behaviors that are motivated by the person's over-all concerns. For example, one of the motives for choosing to become angry rather than to see the other as irresponsible is the angry person's requirement to be in a close relationship with the other. Anger, like any emotion, functions in the service of the activities to which the person is committed.

But this way of comprehending emotion raises an important question. If anger may be regarded as an activity that, like other behavior, is directed and is motivated by the person's concerns, how does it differ from willed behavior—from action that is projected by the person, motivated by his various concerns, and for which the person takes responsibility (see Ricoeur, 1966)? The crucial difference is that the person has neither the freedom to imaginatively project his behavior nor the feeling of responsibility for the behavior. He is the moved rather than the mover, although in both cases it is his under-lying caring, his concerns, that are at the heart of the move-ment.

Rather than attributing the activity to the self, the activity of emotion is experienced as required by the world. It is this world that confronts us with challenges, with goodness, evil, and delight; it is this world that gives us success or failure, suddenly confronts us with the fulfillment of a wish or a loss that seems more than we can bear. Emotions are transforma-tions of our relation to this world. Given our concerns, these transformations are required by the nature of the world. To return to our earlier example: given McPherson's concerns—to stop Deborah's taunting behavior and to treat her with respect—the fact of Deborah's intransigence *requires* McPher-son to get angry. He *has* to get angry if he is to maintain the integrity of his concerns.

In summary, anger and all other emotions function to advance the person's concerns by adjusting the relation between the person and whatever his world confronts him with. Each different emotion deals with a different set of cir-cumstances posed by the world.

THE CHARACTERIZATION OF AN EMOTION'S STRUCTURE

Our examination of anger suggests that any emotion may be characterized in the following ways:

1. As a particular way of perceiving the situation in which the person finds himself. Thus, anger always involves the perception of a challenge to what the person asserts ought to exist. This perception of the situation is actually a transaction between the person and the environment involving a number of choices which give meaning to whatever occurs. As we have seen, one could choose to distance the other rather than to see his behavior as a challenge, or one could choose to become depressed and fail to assert what ought to be.

2. As a response to this perception, a response involving a movement or transformation of the person's relationship with the other (or implicit other). This response can be characterized as an instruction that directs the relation toward a specific end (e.g., anger's "remove it" or depression's "give it up"). The emotion persists until the situation has been transformed, either by the successful accomplishment of the instruction or a change in the meaning of the situation.

3. As it is expressed by the way in which it transforms the person's body and/or his relation to his environment in a specific way. These transformations are always in the service of the emotion's instruction. Thus, anger strengthens the person's will to assert, while depression weakens the will to prevent assertion of the person's value.

4. As a functional adjustment to the exigencies of the person's total situation. This function may be described by relating the emotion's instruction to other aspects of the person's relations with his self and others. Thus, while anger removes the challenge it preserves the unit with the other; while depression sacrifices the person's position it maintains his values.

In fact, each of these four ways in which an emotion may be characterized is an aspect of the psychological organization that is the emotion. That is, an emotion is a whole, a gestalt, and we have been describing four interrelated parts of its structure. One cannot really separate the emotion's response (e.g., removal) from its way of perceiving the situation (a challenge, which is something to be removed). One cannot actualize this response—the emotion's instruction—without the particular transformation of the body and its relation to the environment that characterizes the emotion's expression (one cannot remove a challenge without a strengthened will). Finally, the entire organization would not exist were it not motivated by the way in which it functions to affect relations in the broader scheme of the person's projects and inter-personal relations (the perception of a challenge that can be removed functions to maintain the unit with the other in which the person's values are manifested and, hence, avoids having to create distance). Thus, any emotion may be conceptualized as a structure that is composed of a set of transformations that alter the person's body and its relations with the environment, transformations that carry out an instruction that changes the situation in which the person perceives himself, an instruction that functions to advance the projects to which he is committed.

As a working hypothesis we may assert that any particular species of emotion (anger, esteem, wonder, etc.) may be characterized by its own particular structure and described by specifying its situation, its transformations (instructions and bodily expression), and its function. These structures may be described with a high degree of specificity that reveals intriguing psychological dynamics and enables us to make precise distinctions between closely related emotions. This structural approach has been used by Goodman (1975) to distinguish the emotion of anxiety from the emotions of panic, fear, terror, and apprehension, and by Lindsay (1975) to distinguish between the emotions of joy, elation, and gladness. As an example, let us briefly contrast these last two emotions. In the case of elation, we find that the emotion occurs as a response to a situation in which the person experiences that a *wish* has been fulfilled. In order to realize this wish—to really believe that what was on the level of fantasy is now reality—the person must go up to the fantasy level. The person experiences himself as lifted, and this highness takes him out of contact with those around him. On the other hand, gladness occurs when *hope* is fulfilled. As described by Marcel (1967), a hope differs from a wish by being grounded in the person's reality. The realization of a hope does not require the person to go "up." However, hoping always entails dependency and some doubt about whether this is justified. The dispelling of this doubt results in the brightening of gladness, the emotion enabling the person to reaffirm his dependency. A knowledge of these characteristics of elation and gladness, inherent in the structures of the emotions, is important in understanding how different persons react to common situations. Some persons avoid the experience of elation because they dislike the fact that its "lift" takes them out of contact with the reality of others. Others use elation as a way of rejuvenating themselves. Some welcome gladness and base their life on hope, while others are suspicious of hoping, avoid its implicit dependency, and confuse it with fantasy. Note that this variance, these important differences in how individuals experience emotions, is based on the invariance of the structures of the particular emotions (e.g., the fact that elation always involves being lifted).

Chapter Four

TESTING THE
STRUCTURAL THEORY

We have just seen how any emotion may be understood as a particular structure, an organization of interdependent transformations, which functions to advance the person's concerns by adjusting his relation to the world in which he finds himself. These transformations alter the person's body and its relation to the environment in a specific way that moves the person relative to an other so that the person responds in a functional way to the particular situation in which he finds himself.

However, the structural approach to the emotions assumes not only that it is possible to articulate a unique structure for each emotion, but that these structures are all interrelated parts of a larger system so that it should be possible to specify relations between the various emotions, and to create a language for emotional life that reveals necessary relations between emotions and values in much the same way that geometry reveals necessary relations between points and lines. In Chapter Two, I attempted to demonstrate one aspect of such a system by showing that we could specify the relations between 24 different emotions by postulating a set of four basic choices that may underlie all interpersonal relations. According to the theory, any particular emotion with its unique set of transformations is constituted by these choices (whether the person or an implicit other is the subject of the movement, the movement is toward or away from the other or the person, the movement alters the position of the person or the other, the movement occurs along the dimensions of belonging, recognition, or being). In the case of anger, the transformation—removing a challenge—clearly implies that the person is the subject of a movement that is away from the self, altering the position of the other along the dimension of belonging. And, as we have seen the emotion of depression reflects an identical pattern of choices except that the other is the subject of the movement—so that the self is removed from challenging what ought to be.

In this chapter I shall begin to test this structural theory in three different ways. First, to what extent does it provide us with a unified picture of the emotions that enables us to understand the widely diverse impressions given by the different theories reviewed in the introductory chapter? Second, to what extent does the matrix of 24 emotions account for the wide variance of emotions portrayed by the English language? Third, to what extent is the structure real rather than imposed —to what extent can it systematically help us to understand concrete emotional experience?

ACCOUNTING FOR PHENOMENA
ELUCIDATED BY PREVIOUS THEORIES

The structural theory is compatible with cognitive theory (Beck, 1976) in the sense that it asserts that each emotion occurs in a particular situation with a particular meaning (e.g., a challenge, a loss). However, it emphasizes the transactional nature of this meaning—we speak of the emotion giving the situation the meaning as well as the emotional response being determined by the situation's meaning. And it stresses the fact that this meaning is given in the light of the person's over-all concerns. Thus, it agrees with Angyal's (1941) theory that emotional experience is a symbol, an active organization that captures the implications that a situation has for a person's welfare.

The structural theory is in accord with affective theory in that it asserts that an emotion is not simply a particular way of responding to a particular situation but is literally an imaginative transformation, a restructuring of the relation between the person and the situation. The response of anger, for example—whether it be curses, blows, violent imagery, or a straightforward assertion—is directed at an other who becomes transformed through perception into a leering face, an obstinate fool, or someone or something that is intolerably wrong. And the anger, however it is expressed, transforms the situation so that there is a psychological removal of this challenge to what ought to be. This assertion that emotions are transformations of a person's relation to the world also agrees with the theories advanced by Sartre (1948) and Pribram and Melges (1969). The theory even agrees that emotion occurs when action is not possible. However, whereas Sartre presents emotions as an escape from the realities of a deterministic world, structural theory emphasizes that emotions may occur when action would be impossible because of one's lack of control. This is often true in the magical world of interpersonal relations because the person is dealing with an *other* who may be, quite correctly, perceived as another free agent. Ideally, emotions are not an escape from the world, but rather function to reveal the values of the world—the way in which the person should relate to the other. In this sense, the theory is congruent with Arnold's (1960) presentation of emotions as intimately related to the appraisal of value. However, the emotional response is understood as a transformation rather than as an "action tendency."

The structural theory is also compatible with connative theory in that the instructional transformation of an emotion is related to McDougall's (1908) concept of instinct. The emotion's instruction clearly commands the person to achieve a specific end state relative to the object of the emotion and the emotion persists until this instruction is accomplished, or until a different set of choices gives the situation a different meaning. However, rather than reflecting a fixed quantity of instinctual energy, the emotion's energy is the product of organization (the emotion's structure). In agreement with McDougall, the structural theory depicts emotions as in the service of the person's over-all concerns; however, it conceives of emotional instructions as parts of a system that governs object relations rather than as a set of separate instinctual entities.

The instructional transformation may be fulfilled in two different ways. First, the behavior accompanying the instructional transformation (asserting, attacking, fleeing, approaching, etc.) may result in a change of relative position as either the other or the person withdraws, approaches, or does whatever else is imperative. This is how McDougall (1908), Cannon (1927), Miller (1951), and others conceive of emotion as operating. However, it is important to note that these changes do not necessarily consist of overt movements, such as running. Rather, the emotion may lead to psychological changes that alter behavior. For example, the other may accept responsibility so that he no longer challenges an ought. Second, the expression of the emotion may result in a psychological change in the person. For instance, he may assert his position in a way that is impregnable to challenge by the other, or the symbolic removal of the other may lead to a relief of tension that enables him to see the situation in a different way. This is the sort of "magical" effect that Sartre might stress.

In either case, the emotion—the dynamic organization whose structure we have described—presses toward the specific type of movement that characterizes that emotion. The energic dynamics of this gestalt are quite similar to that of the "tension-systems" that Kurt Lewin describes (see de Rivera, 1976). That is, the emotional organization has a need for completion and will seek substitute satisfaction. And, as Mucchielli (1966) has shown, these structures may persist in unconscious forms which determine broad patterns of behavior in a person's life. The structure of the emotion may even become transformed into an opposite by a sudden change in the choice structure.

However, it is also true that this emotional energy is dependent on the organization—the structure—as a whole. If the situation acquires a different meaning, the organization will break up and the emotion will disappear. For example, if the person discovers that the other's behavior does not challenge his position—was perhaps misunderstood—the entire anger organization will vanish. In this regard, it is crucial to distinguish between defenses, which repress or isolate an emotional structure that is left intact and is still operative; a flexible involvement, which permits the free creation and dissolution of emotional organizations in a way that is appropriate to the situation; and lack of involvement, which avoids the entanglement of emotions at the sacrifice of object relations.

The relation between the instructional transformation and behavior is of especial interest. Like McDougall, I have stressed the fact that part of an emotion is an instruction that calls for behavior that will fulfill that instruction (e.g., "remove the challenge" calls for an assertion or attack that will accomplish the removal). However, as Sartre emphasizes, emotional behavior is not purposive in the same sense that willed behavior is. We do not hit *in order to* remove the challenge. Rather, the hitting is part of the removal. In fact, from Sartre's perspective, the behavior is like a magical incantation — a way of bringing about the transformation that is demanded. He states, "We do not flee in order to take shelter; we flee for lack of power to annihilate ourselves in the state of fainting" (1948, p. 63).

The instructional transformation can only occur in conjunction with the emotion's expressive transformation — the changes in the body and its relation to the environment that make it possible to carry out the instruction. It is this aspect of emotion that has been emphasized by James (1890) and other theorists who stress the role that bodily involvement plays in the emotions. The structural theory agrees that emotion always involves the body but asserts that this is only one part of the emotion's structure. Nevertheless, a change in this part (or any other part) can effect a change in the whole. Performing certain behavior patterns may help produce the instruction (e.g., we start back and then experience fear). And we may be able to change a current emotional organization by encouraging a person to act in ways that are incompatible with the organization's instruction (e.g., we may facilitate the break up of a depression by encouraging the patient to walk [Beck, 1976, pp. 284-286]).

Yet the fact remains that emotional behavior is clearly tied to a particular instruction. Although we can refine our behavior and learn to hit rather than howl, or assert ourselves rather than hit, emotional behavior is not completely malleable. It must be consistent with a specific purpose such as removal or escape. This behavior need not be magical in the sense of being unrealistic, nor reflexive in the sense of being a blind reaction. From the standpoint of structural theory, it is most likely to be an adaptive action that is part of an organization created by the person in order to advance his concerns in the world in which he finds himself. The reason an emotional organization is often adaptive lies in the fact that it is a part of a system that deals with a fundamental aspect of the human world—the fact that persons must interact with others who have a will of their own. Given the dyad as the basic unit of human life, the basic choices—who is going to be the subject of the movement, whose position is to be altered, whether the movement is going to be toward or away—are an inherent aspect of existence.

Since the emotion exists as an organization that relates the person to the world in a particular way, the person may respond to the structure of this organization in its own right. As Tomkins's (1962) theory indicates, the person may find the experience pleasurable or painful and may be motivated to behave in ways that produce or avoid the emotion. The structural theory makes it clear that these are secondary motivational properties which must be distinguished from the emotion's transformations and the behavior associated with these transformations. Thus, the pleasure or pain of anger may have secondary motivational consequences quite apart from the assertive or aggressive behavior involved in accomplishing the instruction to remove the other. Furthermore, precise specification of the structures of particular emotions clarifies exactly what it is that makes the emotion pleasurable or painful to different individuals. As was mentioned, the structure of elation involves a lifting transformation that breaks the person's contact with the reality of others and thereby upsets persons who are concerned with "keeping their feet on the ground."

In many respects the structural theory is compatible with the theory advanced by Hillman (1961). However, the structural theory emphasizes the person's relation to the world whereas Hillman focuses on the transformation of the self that occurs when the potential energy of habits, postures, etc., is converted into emotional energy. Hillman asserts that this process is triggered when a symbol unites the conscious with the unconscious self and is always beneficial in that it promotes the unity of the self (provided only that the energy does not overwhelm the self). From a structural perspective this describes one important way in which emotion occurs in a person's life, but emotional organization is a more general process involved in many different object relations, and it may be either beneficial or detrimental.

While, as the Paulhan-Rapaport theory suggests, an emotional transformation may overwhelm the ego or may be treated as a signal by an ego that is detached from the experience, the structural theory asserts that emotions are a fundamental way of relating the person to the world rather than an instinctual discharge or signal. Since the theory focuses on the functional aspects of emotional transformation and the way emotions relate a person's interests to the world, it blends well with clinical theories that stress both the beneficial aspects of experiencing emotion and the necessity of not holding onto an emotion so that it prevents the free flow of new experience. However, structural theory does not insist that all emotion is good. Emotion is seen as an organization that transforms the person's relation to the world. Such behavior may be mistaken—just as a perception may be incorrect—or it may be used for defensive purposes or in an immature way. The theory, as currently formulated, makes no statements about when emotion is a beneficial part of a person's development.

From the above, it may be seen that the structural theory provides us with a single picture of the emotions which is capable of encompassing the many different aspects of emotion emphasized by prior theories. We have observed that previous theories have tended to concentrate on a very limited set of emotions. Let us turn to a more stringent test of the theory. To what degree can the structural theory account for all the emotions captured by the English language?

ACCOUNTING FOR THE DIFFERENT EMOTIONS NAMED IN ENGLISH

The matrix of emotions presented in Chapter Two (Figure 11) is constructed out of four choices and defines 24 different emotions. The systematic grasp of so many emotions is a unique benefit that the structural theory provides. But there are hundreds of emotion names and we must inquire as to whether the 24 we have described reflect the complete spectrum of emotional movements or, conversely, represent only a small segment of emotional life. In order to get a completely unbiased list of emotion names, I have compiled all the terms used by previous theorists. We can attempt to fit these terms into the 24 spaces of the choice matrix and may then decide to what extent the meanings of the terms are captured by the matrix and to what extent they fall outside of it and require additions, revisions, or a complete rejection of the system.

Examination of the writings of those theorists who have addressed the issue of classifying the emotions or have presented a list of what they term emotions, provides 247 different emotion names.[1] However, some of these terms appear to be used ordinarily to refer to a type of behavior rather than an emotion (e.g., self-abasement, cruelty), or to some other psychological state (e.g., appetite, duty). Accordingly, the list was given to three judges who were asked to keep terms that might be used to describe feelings but to eliminate those that they did not use or that described actions rather than feelings. At least two of the three judges eliminated 93 of the terms. We thus have a list of 154 terms that are considered to be the names of emotions both by some psychological theorist and at least two out of three intelligent laypersons. While this

[1] The list is compiled from the writings of: Calkins (1910), Davitz (1969), McDougall (1908), Mercier (1936), Nahlowsky (1862), Plutchik (1962), Ruckmick (1936), Shand (1914), Spinoza (1675), Tomkins (1962), and Wundt (1897).

is not a complete list, it does provide a large unbiased sample of the emotions named in the English language. It is interesting to note that 21 of the 24 emotion names we have analyzed are included in the list (the exceptions are esteem, rejection, and security).

By considering the movement of the emotion designated by each of the 154 terms, we can attempt to place each term in one of the 24 spaces provided by the choice matrix. If we find that this is possible to do, we may conclude that the network of meanings provided by the matrix is broad enough to encompass the major varieties of emotion. Table 9 shows that in fact it is possible to place all 154 terms in the matrix without greatly distorting the meanings of any of the terms.

Some of the terms in Table 9 have multiple meanings. For example, "pity" may be used either in a positive sense that is akin to sympathy or in a negative sense that is close to contempt; "hate" may be used to mean strong dislike or to designate a virulent form of anger. Since there is little to be gained by using pity as a synonym for sympathy or hate as a synonym for dislike, I have chosen the usages that seem more unique. When there are a number of meanings, the placement of terms in the matrix defines the meaning of the terms and makes it clear which usage is being chosen.

While each of the terms has been placed as carefully as possible, I do not claim that my choices are necessarily correct. It is possible that I have failed to identify correctly an emotion's movement, particularly when the emotion is one of the many I have not examined closely. However, my analyses are not completely idiosyncratic. A check on word usage, that will be described later in detail, shows that my choices agree with those of the average subject at least 80 percent of the time.

Having seen that the network of meanings provided by the choice matrix is *wide* enough to enable us to place all of the emotion terms within it, we must inquire as to whether the net is *fine* enough to distinguish between all the shades of meanings provided by the various terms. If it were, then all the terms within each of the 24 spaces would essentially be synonymous. Of course, no two terms have precisely the same

TABLE 9
PLACEMENT OF 154 EMOTION NAMES IN THE FOUR-CHOICE MATRIX

Subject's position altered	TOWARD					
	Belonging		Recognition		Being	
	Love		*Esteem*		*Acceptance*	
Person as subject (active)[a]	affection benevolence devotion	love protectiveness tenderness	approval gratitude respect	reverence thankfulness	acceptance friendliness	liking sympathy
	Security		*Humility*		*Serenity*	
Other as subject (passive)	contentment cheerfulness freedom	happiness relief	dignity "gratified" humility	modesty "moral" patience	complacence pensiveness resignation	satisfaction serenity

a Note that "active" is not merely a synonym for the person's being the subject of the movement, but rather depends on the interaction between who is the subject of the movement and whose position is altered.

TABLE 9 — *Continued*

	TOWARD		
Object's position altered	Belonging	Recognition	Being
Person as subject (passive)	*Desire* craving lust desire nostalgia inclination passion jealousy	*Admiration* admiration envy	*Wonder* amazement interest amusement perplexity astonishment surprise awe wonder curiosity
Other as subject (active)	*Confidence* ambition excitement confidence "expectant" courage hope determination "inspired" eagerness "powerful" enthusiasm "willful"	*Pride* exultation triumph pride vanity "successful" virtue superiority	*Joy* delight gaiety ecstasy joy elation pleasure enjoyment rapture "frolicsome"

		AWAY		
		Belonging	Recognition	Being
Object's position altered	Person as subject (active)	*Anger* anger annoyance "disagreeable" exasperation frustration fury hate impatience indignation irritation "malice" "oppressed" rage resentment vexation	*Contempt* contempt pity scorn	*Rejection* abhorrence aversion disgust dislike loathing nausea
	Other as subject (passive)	*Depression* apathy "blasé" boredom "defeated" dejection depression despondency helplessness "melancholy" sadness timidity weakness	*Shame* humiliation inferiority "ludicrous" meekness "mortified" shame (ashamed)	*Sorrow* anguish despair disappointment discontent distress grief pain isolation loneliness sorrow
Subject's position altered	Person as subject (passive)	*Fear* alarm fear (afraid, frightened) "restrained" terror worry	*Horror* dismay horror	*Dread* apprehension disbelief doubt dread skepticism suspicion
	Other as subject (active)	*Anxiety* anxiety distraction nervousness	*Guilt* embarrassment guilt regret remorse repentence	*Panic* panic startle "strange"

meaning, for without at least connotative differences one of the words would drop out of the language. However, a structural analysis is interested in denotative meaning and in this regard some of the terms in Table 9 do appear to be synonymous. Contempt and scorn, for instance, seem to refer to the same emotion, as do afraid and frightened.

Still, many of the terms within each space seem to have noticeably different meanings (e.g., guilt and embarrassment) and, in general, a structural analysis is committed to the articulation of any qualitative difference in the experience of two different emotions. When different terms exist there are usually such qualitative differences. For instance, at first glance it might be thought that anger and hate refer to different degrees of intensity of the same emotion. However, reflection indicates that the movements have different qualities and should ideally be distinguished by a structural analysis.

Using such stringent criteria, an inspection of Table 9 shows that the net provided by the matrix is clearly not fine enough — many crucial differences between emotions are not captured by the mesh of a structure with only 24 spaces. We must therefore inquire as to whether it might be possible to specify other choices which could help us to discriminate between the terms within each of the 24 spaces. Needless to say, if there are such choices, they should reflect interesting aspects of psychological processes.

THE FLUID-FIXED CHOICE

Examination of the emotions within each of the spaces of Table 9 reveals an interesting difference in the quality of the movement exhibited by some of the different emotions. This difference is illustrated by the difference between anger and hate.

Either anger or hate may be expressed in a person's behavior. However, the behavior of anger reflects that the persons feels that there is something he can do about his anger. The behavior is aimed at fulfilling the emotion's instruction and thus relieves the anger. The movement occurs as the person acts to achieve his wish. The behavior of hate, on the other hand, is not really directed at fulfilling the instruction to remove the other, for there is nothing that can really be done to achieve this. Even if the other is destroyed, the memory of the evil that he stood for persists and the emotion itself does not really move. We describe hate as "icy" or as "frozen rage," and any feeling of heat is "stifling." These differences are, of course, reflected in the person's perception of the other. In anger, there is a feeling that the other has *acted* in a bad way, whereas in hate there is a feeling that the other *is* evil. Thus, in anger there is a simple desire to remove the other, while in hate the person may wish for the other to suffer. An analogous difference separates disapproval (which flows) and disrespect (which is static).

In the case of the positive emotions we find this same distinction. Approval flows freely toward an other who behaves in an exemplary way, while respect has a static quality and is directed at the other's character rather than simply his behavior. The experience of admiration implies that we can potentially be like the person whom we admire, whereas in envy there is no way we can be in the other's position.

Once an emotion is established, the situation to which it is responsive seems so evident it is hard to imagine how the situation could be otherwise and, hence, how a choice has been made. This is particularly true if we contrast a flowing with a static emotion. A hypothetical example may help to illustrate the basic choice process. Suppose some people at a party observe that one of the guests urinates in his pants and it is inferred that the guest has been drinking too heavily. Then some of the observers may feel contempt for this guest. Their feeling of contempt reflects the pattern of choices that constitute pushing this guest away from what they themselves are like. In essence they are saying, "Though that guest may superficially resemble me he is really not anything like the dignified, controlled person I am."

But now let one of the observers remark that the guest has not been drinking at all, but is the unfortunate victim of a bladder dysfunction. What are the contemptuous observers going to do? They cannot shove away an unfortunate victim of bladder dysfunction, for this is not the victim's fault and their conscarences do not permit such disregard for a fellow human. Still, an uppermost thought in their minds is that they do not want to be like this person. So the choice pattern to shove away the likeness of this man remains the same except that a choice is made to inhibit the movements otherwise called for. As a result there is a slightly different choice pattern and the observers feel the emotion of pity. (Needless to say, this feeling of pity is a negative feeling that is not at all like the feeling of sympathy.)

In the case of the me emotions, it is the self whose behavior or character is at issue, the self toward whom the other can move with ease or difficulty. For example, the emotion of embarrassment presents a person who feels that he is not responsible for his behavior, while guilt presents a person who is responsible and, hence, whose character is at stake. The expression of embarrassment fulfills its instruction ("do not take my behavior to be me—that was unintentional"), whereas guilt is relieved only by atonement and forgiveness.

In the one case the emotional organization is a fluid situation in which it is easy for the emotion's instruction to be realized while in the other there is a relationship, a fixed situation with a more persisting emotion. I shall designate the choice underlying these two types of structures the "fluid-fixed" choice. The emotions resulting from a fixed choice are often experienced as more intense. By contrasting this quality and whether the emotion's movement is fluid or fixed, I have attempted to divide the emotions within each of the 24 spaces into those reflecting a fluid and those reflecting a fixed choice. This gives us the 48-space matrix shown in Table 10.

An inspection of Table 10 shows that the new distinction appears to successfully discriminate between the emotions in most of the spaces. We have increased the resolving power of our matrix so that at least half of the 48 spaces now contain only one term or terms that are relatively synonymous. However, still further discriminations are called for. This is particularly true in the spaces labeled confidence, joy, depression, and grief. In the latter space emotions as dissimilar as disappointment and discontent, and grief and loneliness are still grouped together and obviously demand finer

TABLE 10
PLACEMENT OF EMOTION NAMES IN A FIVE-CHOICE MATRIX

			TOWARD	
		Belonging	Recognition	Being
Subject's position altered				
Person as subject (active)	Fluid	*Love* — affection, benevolence, devotion; love, protectiveness, tenderness	*Esteem* — approval, gratitude; thankfulness	*Acceptance* — acceptance, friendliness; liking, sympathy
	Fixed		respect, reverence	
Person as object (passive)	Fluid	*Security* — cheerfulness, contentment, freedom; happiness, relief	*Humility* — "gratified", patience	*Serenity* — complacence, satisfaction
	Fixed		dignity, humility; modesty, "moral"	pensiveness, resignation, serenity
Object's position altered				
Person as subject (passive)	Fluid	*Desire* — craving, desire; inclination, lust	*Admiration* — admiration	*Wonder* — amazement, amusement, astonishment, interest; perplexity, surprise, wonder
	Fixed	jealousy, nostalgia; passion	envy	awe

TABLE 10—*Continued*

TOWARD

Object's position altered		*Confidence*		*Pride*		*Joy*	
Other as subject (active)	Fluid	ambition, confidence, courage, determination, eagerness, enthusiasm	excitement, "expectant", "inspired", "powerful", "willful"	exultation, pride	"successful", triumph	delight, elation, enjoyment	"frolicsome", gaiety, pleasure
	Fixed	hope		superiority, vanity	virtue	ecstasy, joy	rapture

AWAY

Object's position altered		*Belonging* — *Anger*		*Recognition* — *Contempt*		*Being* — *Rejection*	
Person as subject (active)	Fluid	anger, annoyance, "disagreeable", exasperation, frustration, fury	impatience, indignation, irritation, rage, vexation	contempt	scorn	aversion, disgust	dislike, nausea
	Fixed	hate, "oppressed", resentment	"malice"	pity			abhorrence, loathing

Object's position altered		*Depression*		*Shame*		*Sorrow*	
Other as subject (passive)	Fluid	"blasé" boredom "defeated" "dejection"	restraint sadness timidity weakness	humiliation "ludicrous"	"mortified" shame (ashamed)	disappointment discontent	distress pain sorrow
	Fixed	apathy depression despondency	helplessness "melancholy"	inferior	meekness	anguish despair grief	isolation loneliness

		Fear		*Horror*		*Dread*	
Person as subject (passive)	Fluid	alarm	fear (afraid, frightened)	dismay		apprehension disbelief doubt	skepticism suspicion
	Fixed	terror		horror		dread	

Subject's position altered		*Anxiety*		*Guilt*		*Panic*	
Other as subject (active)	Fluid	distraction nervousness	"restrained" worry	embarrassment	repentence regret		"startle"
	Fixed	anxiety		guilt	remorse	panic	"strange"

analysis. This is not an easy task because the demand for parsimony requires us to find a choice that will also be useful in discriminating between other emotions in the matrix. A possible sixth choice is briefly described in Appendix B but I am no longer happy with the rationale for the choice. Still other possible choices are considered in a preliminary investigation by Lau (1974). He focuses on a set of 18 terms that may be placed in the space labeled joy and articulates a series of dimensions that may be used to distinguish the different feelings within that space. Before any further analysis it seems desirable to systematically collect all of the terms for emotions in the English language. (There are probably about 500 such terms.) Since the over-all power of the structural theory to discriminate between different emotions is clear, rather than attempting any further distinctions in this monograph, I shall turn to several other issues that may be raised.

The 48 spaces created by the additional distinction between fluid and fixed emotions contain the name of an emotion in all but three cases (the fixed choice equivalents of love, acceptance, and security). The structural theory must suppose that such emotions exist and it seems probable that they would be referred to in the English language. A search through Roget's *Thesaurus* uncovered three terms that appear to be names for the emotions that fit these spaces and were probably simply overlooked by previous investigators. The terms — adoration, compassion, and faith — appear to refer to fixed emotions whose choice structure is in all other respects comparable to the emotions of love, acceptance, and security respectively. Thus, we may feel compassion for what we cannot accept, and while security is dependent on some expression of love, the essence of faith is its persistence in the face of apparent abandonment.

THE RELIABILITY OF USAGE OF EMOTION NAMES

While I personally find it easy to place the large majority of emotion terms within spaces in the choice matrix we must inquire into the reliability of these placements. Do persons agree with each other as to where to put each word and, if so, would the majority of these placements agree with the ones I have indicated? One way to assess this would be to have a number of persons read Chapter Two and then act as a panel of judges and indicate where they agree and where they disagree (or had questions) about the placement of each term. Such a procedure should reveal any weaknesses inherent in the theory, in its exposition, and in my own placement of emotion terms. However, this procedure would require sophisticated judges and a good deal of time. Moreover, it would be open to the charge that the judges were biased by seeing my own placements. Consequently a completely different procedure was used. Twenty college students who were not at all acquainted with the theory were given the list of emotion terms, a brief description of one of the choices, and a few examples of which emotion names were used with each choice. Then each student was asked to privately make a choice of usage for every term on the list. On succeeding days the same group of subjects was given a different choice to make until each had made the series of five choices for every emotion name. The full details of this procedure, including the descriptions of the choices, the example words, and data on individual differences in the ability to use the words, are given in Appendix B. The complete list of terms and the choice data are presented in Appendix C.

The first question we may ask of these date is whether or not the subjects agree at all on how emotion words should be used. If their answers are completely idiosyncratic then we would expect a chance distribution of answers. Such a result would indicate either that emotion terms have completely private or ambiguous meanings, that the descriptions of the choices are inadequate, or that the structural theory is incorrect in positing that the choices exist. However, if at least 15 of the 20 subjects agree on how a term is used, we may be fairly certain that some norm is operating. Such results would occur by chance only 4.2 times out of 100.[2] Second, if we work only with those words where the subjects show a significant agreement with one another, we may ask whether their agreement

---

[2] This degree of chance is calculated by expanding the binomial $(\frac{1}{2} + \frac{1}{2})^{20}$ and considering both ends of the distribution.

conforms to my own choices inherent in the placement of the words in Table 10. Here a lack of conformity indicates either that there is a lack of precision in the descriptions of the choices or that the choices do not really govern the term's usage. Finally, with somewhat less rigor, we may ask whether or not a majority of the subjects agree with my own choices. Of course, we may assess the degree of conformity for each of the five choices that have been described. The results of these statistical analyses are shown in Table 11. To avoid any bias, when words were used as examples they were excluded from the data.

Table 11 demonstrates that for every choice there is agreement as to how at least half of our emotion terms are used and that this usage usually conforms to the choices that have been specified. For example, in the case of 68 percent of our emotion names there is significant agreement among persons as to whether the person or the other is the subject of the emotion. When this agreement exists, 98 percent of the names conform to the usage specified in Table 10. And, considering all of the emotion names, 88 percent of the time the author's choice as to whether the term refers to an it or a me emotion is concurred with by a majority of the subjects.

The figures in Table 11 suggest that the descriptions for the first three choices are reasonably adequate and that the usage of over 90 percent of our emotion terms may be described in terms of these choices. However, in the case of the belonging-recognizing-being choice and the fluid-fixed choice, there is room for improvement. Either these two choices are only applicable to 60 to 70 percent of our emotion terms or the description of the choices needs to be stated with more precision. The relatively low degree of agreement between the subjects and the author (73 percent, 76 percent) suggests that the descriptive statements used to convey the nature of these choices need to be improved. Until this is attempted we cannot really be sure whether the choices are less fundamental or are simply more difficult to convey. However, even as the choices are currently stated, they may be used successfully to distinguish the usages of between 50 and 70 percent of our emotion names.

TABLE 11
PERCENTAGE OF EMOTION NAMES WHOSE USAGE CAN BE RELIABLY SPECIFIED

Choice	It-Me	Toward-Away	Subject Moves-Object Moves	Belonging-Recognition-Being	Fluid-Fixed
Percent of emotion names where the choice is agreed upon by a significant[a] number of subjects	68	89	63	57	54
Percent of emotion names with significant agreement among subjects that agree with the author's usage	98	99	100	73	76
Percent of emotion names where a majority of subjects agreed with the author's usage	88	97	92	57	71

[a] Judged significant when at least 15 of 20 subjects agreed (.042 level, two-tailed) or, in the case of three-way choice, when at least 12 of the subjects agreed (.08 level, two-tailed).

ACCOUNTING FOR EMOTIONAL EXPERIENCE

We have seen how our picture of the emotions as transformational structures can unify the various aspects of the emotions explained by previous theories. And it seems clear that the structural theory is relatively successful in accounting for a large number of these emotional structures by relating them to a simple set of choices which appear to be an inherent aspect of one person's being in relation to another. However, the crucial question that must be asked is whether the structure presented is really inherent in emotional experience or whether it is simply a useful fiction imposed on our experience. Previous theories have portrayed the emotions as either relatively separate entities or as a mush of mixed-up bodily sensations. Are emotions really parts of a system that interrelates all aspects of object relations? What research can help us to either verify or abandon the assertion that emotional experiences are transformations that are aspects of a *system*—that experience is far more structured than has been previously realized? At least three directions must be explored: (1) elucidation of the structures of individual emotions and the attempt to establish logical relations between these structures, (2) investigation of exactly when an emotion occurs within the life of an individual and the role the emotion plays in preventing or aiding personal development, and (3) exploration of cross-cultural differences and similarities in the ways emotions are experienced and used to relate the individual and society. Let us briefly consider each of these directions for future research.

ESTABLISHING PRECISE RELATIONS BETWEEN STRUCTURES

On the one hand, structural theory encourages an exploration of the concrete experience of particular emotions and the attempt to elucidate the peculiarities of their structures. Goodman's (1975) research distinguishing between the experiences of anxiety, panic, fear, terror, and apprehension; Lindsay's (1975) work explicating different structures for joy, elation, and gladness; Kane's (1976) attempt to isolate depression from sadness, grief, and guilt; Funk's (1974) articulation of the structure of the different types of laughter; and Kreilkamp's (1970) distinctions between types of psychological distance often yield surprising insights into the structure of experience so that patterns which would otherwise be overlooked are recognized and hidden relations become apparent. This research increases our sensitivity to emotional experience and enables us to perceive what would otherwise go unnoticed.

On the other hand, since the theory sees all emotions as parts of one interrelational system, it encourages an attempt to relate all the concepts involved in clarifying individual emotions, an attempt to create an abstract system of relations—a geometry of psychological choices. These two endeavors help balance each other; the one keeping the investigator in contact with the concrete reality of experience, the other leading the investigator to ask questions that would not otherwise occur and to demand a creative way of viewing the ordinary. Nevertheless, there is bound to be tension between these two poles—the one insisting that the investigator be faithful to experience, the other requiring the sparse elegance of precise relations between a few abstract constructs. One of the best tests of structural theory is whether it can continue to parsimoniously relate the structures of particular emotions as these structures become more precisely specified.

As more knowledge is acquired about the details of the structures of particular emotions, it will be necessary to establish relations between these details and this will inevitably force revisions of the over-all choice structure. Already our knowledge of particular emotions demands more precise statements about the nature of the dimensions of psychological space. For example, it seems clear that the person feels lifted up in elation and pressed down in depression. These are not just idle metaphors. Research demonstrates that the person actually perceives the horizon differently, locating it lower when he is "high" and placing it higher when he is "down" (Wapner, Werner, and Krus, 1957). Furthermore, the person actually is somewhat out of contact with others, who remain on the horizontal plane where an other can be met (Jager, 1971). We also know that in euphoria the person expands while in depression he contracts. Again these are not whimsical terms. The person's verbosity and even the amount of space taken up by his handwriting shows this expansiveness or constriction (Johnson, 1938). Such changes occur on the horizontal rather than the vertical plane of psychological space.

If the structural theory is correct in its assertion that the emotions are systematically interrelated, it should be able to demonstrate precise relations between these emotions and between the dimensions of horizontal and vertical. Yet the current choice matrix fails to do this. True, it hints that the belonging emotions are associated with the horizontal, the recognition emotions with the vertical, and the being emotions with depth. But this fails to account for the vertical dimension of an emotion such as elation which is concerned with being. We cannot really be confident that the over-all structure is inherent, rather than imposed, until it establishes a network of relations that enables us to give a more precise account of the characteristics of particular emotional structures.

SPECIFYING WHEN EMOTION OCCURS
AND ITS ROLE IN DEVELOPMENT

According to the structural theory, emotion occurs when activity cannot be initiated by the self but instead is required by the world, which confronts the person with a *fait accompli* affecting his interests (a challenge, a success or failure, a danger, goodness, evil). The emotion is the transformation of our relation to this world, the transformation that is required to deal with this change in the world. However, there are many times when we are confronted by sudden events that affect our interests and yet produce willed activity rather than emotion. We need to be able to specify the exact conditions under which emotion will occur. If the structural theory is correct, these conditions must be related to the dissolution of the person's self-boundary and this must, in turn, be related to the existence of the dyad as the unit of behavior and, hence, the structure of choices that have been specified. To establish these conditions, we shall have to add a dynamic dimension to structural inquiry; we shall have to study concrete occurrences of emotion in the context of an individual's life.

Preliminary investigation in this area reveals enormous individual differences in the ways persons experience emotions in their life. For example, some persons tend to experience emotions as single entities which may succeed each other in rapid sequence, while others ordinarily experience emotions in simultaneous clusters or mixtures. Some are sensitive to qualitative differences in feelings and can easily discriminate between feelings as closely related as tenderness, affection, and fondness. Others appear to be almost "feeling blind" and can no more distinguish the feeling of fear from the feeling of anger than a color-blind person can tell red from green. Such individual differences are even more striking when persons are asked to describe the role that emotions play in their lives. In one group discussion, a person remarked that she saw herself as ". . . the weaver of my life. The emotions are red and yellow threads which, interwoven with the ordinary whites and grays, add color to enrich the cloth." Hearing this remark another responded, "Why I'm not like that at all. My life, like the world, is filled with mountains, plains, swamps and deserts; the emotions are winds which pick me up from a swamp and deposit me on a mountain top or set me in a desert." This difference in how emotions are experienced naturally affects the importance assigned to the emotions in one's life. One person explains, "My life is like that of a city. Many things are happening—industry is progressing, commerce flourishes, ball games are played. The emotions are rather like the weather. They always affect the city to some extent, particularly the parks, but they don't ordinarily govern the life of the city." Contrast such a view with that presented by Bertrand Russell in his autobiography: "Three passions, simple but overwhelmingly strong, have governed my life: the longing for love, the search for knowledge, and unbearable pity for the suffering of mankind. These passions, like great winds, have blown me hither and thither, in a wayward course, over a deep ocean of anguish, reaching to the very verge of despair" (1967, prologue).

Given such differences, one may suspect that one of the reasons we have so many incompatible theories about the emotions is that different investigators experience their own emotions quite differently. In one of his essays on the emotion of love, Ortega y Gasset mentions, ". . . there are two irreducible kinds of men: those who experience happiness as a feeling of being outside of themselves, and those who, on the contrary, feel fulfilled only when self-possessed" (1957, p. 69). Since emotions often involve being "outside" the self rather than being self-possessed, we might inquire whether this Dionysian-Apollonian difference accounts for some theorists seeing emotions as the source of life while others view the emotional as a disruptive plague. In any case, it is clear that investigations into the conditions under which an emotion occurs must consider the different roles that emotion may play in the person's life.

CROSS-CULTURAL STUDIES AND THE
RELATION OF LANGUAGE TO EXPERIENCE

We have been relying on words that are used to refer to emotions (emotion "names") in order to stimulate the recall of different emotions so that we may compare their characteristics. And we have seen that these words are, by and large, used in ways that conform to the postulates of the structural theory. However, we are interested in the experience of emotions and not simply words. Our reliance on language raises a number of interesting questions about the role of language in organizing our experience. On the one hand, it seems that our experience is always mediated by language, that different languages organize experience in different ways, and that every language is an interpretation of reality that stresses certain features, ignores others, and channels our way of experiencing the world. On the other hand, there seems to be a reality that is independent of language. Though our experience is dependent on language and is but a construction, it is not a fantasy, it is an *interpretation* of reality. And although each language organizes emotional reality somewhat differently (the French *joi* is not exactly the same as the English *joy*), we expect that emotions are somehow universal and the structural theory asserts that emotions in all cultures reflect the same basic psychological processes (though this idea too must be expressed in language).

But is this really so? Do the emotions experienced by persons from a different culture really correspond to those portrayed by the English language? One advantage of the structural theory is that it allows us to test whether or not this is so. We can ask whether or not the emotion terms of other languages can be systematically related to a common structure of processes.[3] While the answer to this question requires a great deal of systematic investigation, I have been encouraged by the description of emotions in works on the Japanese culture (Doi, 1973), the Utku eskimoes (Briggs, 1970), and the Gahuku tribes of New Guinea (Read, 1965). Each of these works is interesting for unique reasons: Doi addresses himself to the fact that the Japanese have an emotion that is not named in English; Briggs provides a glossary of Utku emotion terms that are clearly organized in a way that is somewhat different from English; and Read provides examples of emotional behavior that are not named within the Gahuku culture. Let us briefly consider each of these findings in turn.

It is not unusual to find individual words in other languages that express shades of meaning that cannot easily be translated into English. For instance, it takes several English words to explain that the German *Schadenfreude* refers to the particular type of pleasure a person may feel when someone whom they dislike meets with a misfortune. (The term is

[3] Anyone interested in this question will want to consider the techniques developed by Osgood, May, and Miron (1975). They have established that three connotative dimensions—evaluation (good-bad), potency (strong-weak), and activity (active-passive)—are indigenous to all human cultures. By translating 620 concepts (including 20 emotion names) into 30 different languages and having native speakers judge these concepts on the three connotative dimensions, they have compiled an atlas of "affective meanings" which enables us to compare the connotative meanings that a concept has in different cultures (for example, how good or bad the concept of hope is judged to be). Of course, this is not a test for denotative similarities (for whether "hope" really has the same structure as the concepts into which it is translated in different languages). However, it is possible to test whether different denotative features predict connotative patterns. In a separate attempt to test denotative features, Osgood has also experimented with a technique using semantic anomalies in different cultures.

usually used as a reproach for such uncharitable wishing.) However, in this case, as in most cases, it is easy for an English-speaking person to recognize what is being referred to, and often there is even a closely related term. For example, I would say that *Schadenfreude* is a type of malicious "glee" (which fits within the matrix space labeled "joy" but which has to be further distinguished). While the average German is undoubtedly more conscious of *Schadenfreude* (since he has a term for the experience), I doubt that he experiences much more of this emotion than the average American does.

On the other hand, in the case Doi discusses, the Japanese language has a term—*amae*—to refer to an emotion that is quite common in the experience of the average Japanese yet is not named in English and is less likely to occur as an emotion in our experience. Furthermore, there is a whole network of other Japanese terms whose meanings have to do with the meaning of *amae* and whose meanings can only be grasped through an understanding of *amae*. Here we are confronted with an emotional difference that is an aspect of the Japanese experience and distinguishes it from the experience of the English-speaking person. It is obviously important for us to understand this emotion of *amae* and to ascertain whether it can be related to the structure that has been described or is so different that it requires a different structure and thus indicates that emotions are more dependent on our linguistic culture than we have hitherto realized.

The emotion of *amae* refers to the wish to lean on another's good will, to be dependently self-indulgent—just as a puppy expects to nurse on its mother. It is in direct opposition to the Western ideal of self-reliance. To the average American (or at least to the average American male) such helpless dependency is positively shameful; the culture discourages it in every possible way. However, the Japanese culture legitimizes this dependency by building it into the normative structure of adult relations. In marriage, and in every other relation, the partners are expected to have *amae* for one another. Consequently the emotion is not only recognized but is encouraged and a whole vocabulary has been built about it: *suneru* is the sulkiness that occurs when one is not allowed to be straightforwardly self-indulgent; *hinekureru* is behaving in a perverse way that feigns indifference to the other instead of showing *amae*; *uramu* is the type of hostility that occurs when one's *amae* is rejected.

This does not mean that *amae* does not exist in the United States. In fact, Doi asserts that *amae* is the equivalent of the dependency that Balint (1952) discovered in his patients and terms "passive object love." And once one becomes sensitive to *amae* one sees it evidenced in all kinds of behavior (e.g., the American male's imperious "When is dinner going to be ready?"). But does it exist as a specific feeling—as an emotion? I believe that it does but is often masked under the general rubric of "love." Doi states that, ". . . the prototype of *amae* is the infant's desire to be close to the mother . . . [it is] . . . the attempt to deny the fact of separation that is such an inseparable part of human existence . . ." (p. 75). In short, I believe that it is precisely the emotion that is concerned with having the other belong to one and which I, lacking the term *amae*, had to label "desire." (In fact, probably *amae* is often a component of sexual desire or longing.) In a sense it is passive rather than active love.

When we turn to Briggs's glossary of Utku emotion terms, I believe we find an equivalent distinction. This Eskimo language distinguishes the emotion *unga* from *naklik*. The former refers to the desire to be in the presence of a loved person. When a child cries at the absence of a parent, doesn't want to go to school or sleep by himself, he is said to *unga*. On the other hand, *naklik* refers ". . . to the desire to feed someone who [is] hungry, warm someone who [is] cold, and protect someone who [is] in danger of physical injury" (p. 320). As one father remarks of his daughter, "She makes one feel naklik; she ungas me very much" (p. 321). Interestingly, the Utku, who indulge their children with affection until about the age of four and then place a number of grown-up emotional demands upon them, seem to regard *unga* with the same openness that the Japanese regard *amae* as long as the emotion occurs in parent-child relations. However, they express it with reluctance when it occurs between spouses.

An even more dramatic illustration of the universality of particular emotional configurations is provided in Read's account of the Gahuku tribes of New Guinea who often channel emotional expression in various rituals. For example, among the Gahuku there is a strong male dominance that is expressed in a scornful attitude toward women, the beating of wives who do not comply with orders, etc. Ordinarily there is little opportunity for any feminine resentment to be expressed. However, following the severe rites of passage that take boys away from their mothers and transform them into adult males, there is a ritualized occasion in which all the women of the tribe assault the males with sticks and stones in an attack vicious enough to break through the ordinary male superiority.

In this cultural milieu, where we are not entirely surprised to learn that there is no word for love, we nevertheless find love and/or *amae*. Read reports that one day the tribal leader approached him for help. His favorite wife, pregnant with their first child, was experiencing great difficulty with the delivery. Read notes, "He told me simply that Guma must not die, phrasing his words imperatively, 'This woman cannot die,' as though the form of command might help to prevent its happening. He added in his next breath that he did not want to lose her, that his feeling for her, touching his hand to his stomach, killed him inside" (p. 108). Here we note an expression of a belonging emotion which occurs in spite of the absence of any term for love; the tribesman creates a metaphor to realize the emotional organization in his experience.

Such cross-cultural similarities reinforce my belief in a universal structure for emotional experience and the fruitfulness of using language as a way to gain access to the underlying structure. Indeed, it is not often realized that Whorf—best known for his emphasis on how language structures experience—was fully aware of these underlying connections between words. He states, "The very existence of such a common stock of conceptions, possibly possessing a yet unstudied arrangement of its own, does not seem to be greatly appreciated; yet to me it seems to be a necessary concomitant of the communicability of ideas by language; it holds the principle of this communicability, and is in a sense the universal language, to which the various specific languages give entrance" (1956, p. 36).

However, if a universal structure exists it is still not clear *why* it exists and the structural theory will not be fully convincing until it is clear why a dyadic structure is necessary. It may be that Gestalt psychologists are correct in their view that such structures are inherent in physical as well as psychological reality and we shall discover that a similar system governs molecular formation. Or it may be that an over-all emotional structure, such as the proposed system, was evolutionarily advantageous for those species that had to deal with dyadic relations. Or it may be that the structure is not inherent in emotions per se but is a necessary aspect of our unique human ability to experience our emotions and is thus at the core of our capacity to have a self and to experience an other. Certainly the structural theory agrees with Strasser (1970) in asserting that emotions reflect a preobjective structure that is the basis for our knowledge of other persons, is the first source of meaning, and constitutes a precondition of reason. It would be strangely appropriate if emotional experience, with its magical capacity to unite us as human beings, were actually inherent in our human separation from nature.

Appendix A

THE FORMAL SIMILARITY BETWEEN THE THEORIES OF McDOUGALL, MILLER, MARSTEN, AND CANNON

STIMULUS-RESPONSE THEORY

The following set of observations have been made:

1. Rats in a box painted half white and half black did not prefer the black end to the white end.

2. When a rat received a shock in the white end, the rat ran to the black end and escaped the shock.

3. After ten shocks, when a rat was placed in the white end, he ran to the black end, *even when he did not get shocked in the white end.*

4. When the passage to the black end was blocked, the rats (a) urinated, defecated, tensed, crouched, and (b) eventually learned to turn a wheel that opened the passageway (Miller, 1951).

The following demonstration has been performed:

1. Rats in a compartment were trained to escape shock by jumping over a hurdle into the other end of the compartment.

2. The rats then heard a buzzer when they were getting shocked in the center of the compartment: on these trials no hurdle was present and escape behavior was prevented.

3. Later when a hurdle was present and the buzzer was sounded, the rats jumped over the hurdle even when there was no shock in that end of the compartment (May, 1948).

In order to explain these results, Miller (1951) postulated that the shock gave rise to an intervening "fear" response

130

which could be learned to previously neutral cues. The fear response was assumed to also act as a strong stimulus that: (1) would motivate behavior to reduce its strength, (2) could serve as a cue to which overt responses could be learned, (3) would call forth various innate autonomic responses and those learned responses that had reduced the fear in the past. These ideas are summarized in Figure 12.

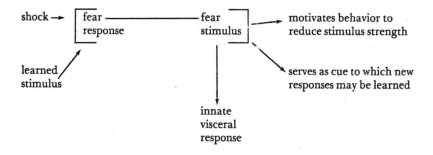

FIGURE 12. Miller's Theory

The postulated fear response appears to handle the facts. In Miller's demonstration, if a fear response occurred when the animal was shocked in the white end of the box, this response could be learned to the white end. Later, even with no shock present, the white end of the box would call forth the fear response and the stimulus properties of the fear response would call forth the observed autonomic responses and moti- vate the learning of new escape behavior to reduce its strength. In May's demonstration the fear response could have acted as a cue to which the hurdle jumping could be learned. Then the fear response would have been learned to the buzzer. Later when the buzzer was presented the fear response would be called forth and in turn stimulate the hurdle-jumping response.

While, thus far, fear is the only emotion that has been sys- tematically treated as an intervening response, other emotions have been roughly designated. Miller (1951) has suggested that anger can be regarded as another intervening stimu- lus-producing response. One of the eliciting conditions would be the frustration of an overt response; the aggression response would be high in the hierarchy of responses to the anger stimulus.

Recently Mowrer (1960) has stated that it is necessary to postulate emotions, represented as intervening variables, in order to predict behavior. He suggests that, as in Miller's demonstration, *fear* may be defined as arising when a danger signal heralds the onset of some noxious stimulus. *Hope* may be defined as arising when a safety signal heralds the disappearance of a noxious stimulus. *Relief* may be postulated to occur when the noxious stimulus disappears. *Disappointment* may occur when the safety signal is not followed by the disappearance of the noxious stimulus.

Miller's and Mowrer's approach to emotion does not appear to be substantially different from McDougall's (1908). A comparison of Figures 12 and 1 shows that when semantic problems are reduced by the schematic diagram, the theories are nearly equivalent. Miller and Mowrer have emphasized, and demonstrated in the laboratory, the importance of the afferent and efferent learning that McDougall speaks of. But in both systems emotion is essentially functional and motivates and guides behavior.

MARSTON'S THEORY

Marston (1928), an early worker in lie detection, has suggested an interesting revision of the James-Lange theory. He points out that the essence of James's (1890) theory is that an emotion is our awareness of our reactions. Since afferent nerves may lead to sensation, and efferent nerves lead to movements but not to sensations, James inferred that our awareness of our reactions must be due to afferent feedback from our reactions. After pointing out that emotions do not feel like sensations, Marston postulates that emotion arises when central motor synapses are active. He states, "Motor consciousness is affective consciousness." Marston accepts the view that conscious emotion follows a reaction, rather than leads to it; but he suggests that emotion is a *direct* awareness of a *central* reaction rather than a complex sensation representing afferent feedback from a peripheral reaction. Marston's theory is schematized in Figure 13.

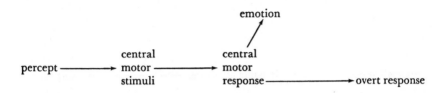

FIGURE 13. Marston's Theory

It should be noted that Marston's theory satisfies Cannon's (1927) criticism of James's theory and is quite compatible with the theories of McDougall and Miller; it merely attempts to be more specific as to how the conscious emotion occurs.

CANNON'S THEORY

Cannon's (1927) theory is based on his criticism of James's theory and on physiological observations of the effects of cortical and thalamic lesions. He proposes that afferent messages prepare the thalamus to be activated, then travel to the cortex where, on the basis of past learning, it is decided whether or not the thalamus should be released from inhibition. If the thalamus is released from inhibition the thalamus sends messages downward to activate skeletal muscles and viscera and upward to the cortex to yield the conscious experience of the emotion. Cannon states: "That the thalamic neurones act in a special combination in a given emotional expression is proved by the reaction patterns typical of the several affective states. These neurones do not require detailed innervation from above in order to be driven into action. Being *released* for action is a primary condition for their service to the body—they then discharge precipitately and intensely" (p. 120).

In a sense, Cannon thought of the thalamus as containing latent emotions. While many physiological psychologists today would relate emotions to the limbic system instead of the thalamus (Brady, 1958), the basic outline of Cannon's thinking is still current. The theory is schematized in Figure 14.

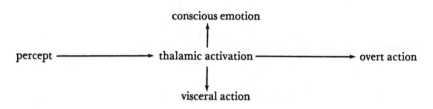

FIGURE 14. Cannon's Theory

It should be noted that this theory is *essentially* the same as those of McDougall, Miller, and Marston. Instead of instincts or central motor responses we have thalamic reaction patterns, but basically the theories are in complete agreement. Furthermore, it is clear that conscious emotion follows, or is part of the expression of, the reaction pattern.

Appendix B

TESTING THE USAGE OF EMOTION NAMES

PROCEDURE

Twenty male students, enrolled in an introductory psychology course at Dartmouth College, volunteered to serve as subjects. They met as a group for approximately one hour on each of six different days.

During each of the six meetings the subjects were instructed in the recognition of the alternatives of one of six choices — the five already described and a sixth to be described below. The subjects then individually considered an alphabetized list of emotion names[1] and judged whether each name was used when one or the other of the alternatives had been decided on. For example, subjects judged whether each emotion name was used when an attraction choice was made or when a repulsion choice was made. If a particular emotion name was not easily referred to an attraction or a repulsion choice, then the subjects would not agree on their judgments and approximately half of the subjects would rate the word as referring to attraction, half to repulsion. If, however, our structural analysis of each emotion is correct, then there should be agreement on how each name was judged.

---

[1] A list of 188 names was used, 141 of the 154 considered in Chapter Four and 47 other names of theoretical interest. The latter are not included in the analyses presented in the text nor in Appendix C. However, they are included in the reliability data presented below.

135

At the end of each session all the judgments were tabulated and the words were divided into groups of names that had all been judged to reflect the same choice. When significant agreement was not reached on the usage of a name, a simple majority vote was used so that the name could be categorized. Occasionally a tie vote occurred; in these instances the experimenter acted as an additional subject and broke the tie. It should be noted that these procedures did not affect the results of a session; they merely ensured that all of the names were divided into groups for the next session.

At the next session the subjects were presented with these groups of names derived from the judgments of the previous session and were given instructions on the recognition of the alternatives of another choice. These instructions were slightly modified to fit the different groups of names. For example, when a group of attraction names were being judged, the instructions for recognizing an extension choice used the concept of giving, whereas when a group of repulsion names were being judged, the instructions for an extension choice used the concept of pushing away.

After each session the names were divided into smaller and smaller groups so that at the end of the sixth session the groups were clusters of a few names that had been judged similarly on all six choices—the synonyms of the analysis.

Several preliminary studies were made in an endeavor to discover the best method of instructing subjects to recognize phenomenally the different choices. It was found that examples of emotions that reflected different choices were invaluable in establishing the meaning of the instructions. It was also apparent that while subjects could understand a theoretical discussion and follow nuances in the instructions, they could not remember complex instructions well enough to apply them easily to a long list of names. Without lengthy training, subjects could only utilize simple, concise instructions.

Although our structural analysis suggests that each of the six choices is made independently of the other decisions, the *recognition* of how one choice has been made often depends on how another choice has been made. If an attraction decision has been made, the extension choice may be recognized by a desire to give to the object, whereas if a repulsion choice has been made, the extension choice may be recognized by a desire to remove the object. Therefore, to maximize accuracy subjects were taught the recognition of some choices before others, and the instructions about later choices varied in accordance with earlier choices.

It is necessary to consider the person-as-subject/other-as-subject choice first because this choice greatly affects how the other choices are recognized. When the person is the subject of the movement, emotion names seem to take an object. Thus, for it emotions the choices lend themselves to a phenomenal analysis of the relation between oneself and the object. On the other hand, when the other is the subject of the movement, the corresponding emotion names do not seem to take an object. For such me emotions, subsequent choices do not yield to an analysis of the relation to an object because no object is phenomenally present. Therefore, the subject has to judge the other choices on the basis of an analysis of the emotion itself. For example, when an object-as-subject choice has been made, a positive choice cannot be felt as an attraction to an outside object. The positive choice is revealed only by the positive tone of the emotion and by the fact that the subject would like to continue feeling the emotion.

The other choices do not have to be considered in any particular order. However, the choice as to whose position is altered follows the attraction-repulsion choice quite naturally and, since both these choices are relatively easy to recognize, they were considered ahead of the remaining three choices. In this way the most difficult choices to recognize were considered later so that the groups of emotion names would be smaller and it would be easier for the subject to contrast the names within each group.

Sets of relatively precise, nontheoretical instructions were prepared for each of the six choices. The complete instructions were read to the subjects and each subject was given a written summary of the instructions that included the emotion names used as examples.

138 JOSEPH DE RIVERA

INSTRUCTIONS

FIRST SESSION: IT-ME CHOICE

We have many different emotions and feelings. Some of these have been given names. The theory of the emotions that we are testing here predicts that you should be able to divide these names into different categories—we use some names in some situations, other names in other situations.

Today I'm going to give you the names of 188 emotions. There are actually several thousand names that refer to emotions but these are the most common ones. All of these names are in the first person. That is, you should put an "I feel" before each of them. The first word is "abhorrence." You are not looking at someone abhorring you. *You* have the feeling. You can say, "I feel abhorrence."

I'm going to ask you to divide these names into two groups according to whether the spotlight is on you or the other person or object. Let me explain what I mean. This is you (draws a circle on the blackboard). This is the other person or object that is causing you to have the emotion (draws an x on the board). Here is a spotlight (draws this). You may be looking at this person or object out here, but the spotlight may be on you or on it (illustrates).

Consider the emotion "contempt": The spotlight is on the other—you would like to do something to him. Consider the emotion "ashamed": The spotlight is on you—shame is about yourself. Consider the emotion "afraid": When you are afraid, you are trying to get away from the other—the spotlight is on him. Consider the emotion "shy": You are describing your-self—the spotlight is on you. Note that you are *looking* at the object out here when you're shy, but the word is about you. You are not really trying to get away from the other; you're trying to overcome something in you. Are there any questions on this distinction?

Consider the emotion "pleased"—"I feel pleased." The spotlight is on it. You're describing how you feel about it. Consider the emotion "encouraged": The spotlight is on you. Of course, the "it" out here may have *caused* you to be encouraged, but you're talking about *yourself*, not about how you feel toward *it*. Is this clear?

To summarize: we use some of these names when we're talking about ourselves and others when we're talking about the object out there that we're dealing with.

Now I'd like you to go over these emotion names very rapidly and write down an *it* or a *me* by each name, according to whether the spotlight is on it or you. I would like you to work rapidly—on first impulse. Always make a judgment one way or the other. The only exception to this is if you do not know what the word means. In that case, write down a question mark. (The subjects begin.)

Summary of Instructions

Emotion names used when talking about: (1) *it*—afraid, contempt, pleased; (2) *me*—ashamed, shy, encouraged.

SECOND SESSION: ATTRACTION-REPULSION CHOICE

Yesterday you judged 188 emotion names on whether you use the word when you are talking about yourself or about somebody else. If there were really no basis for this judgment and you had to make a 50-50 choice as to how you used the word, then we would expect 10 of you to call it a me word and 10 of you to call it an it word. If, on the other hand, there was some basis for the choice, then we would expect a majority to rate the word one way or the other. Statistically there is only one chance in 20 that 15 or more of you would agree on how to rate the word by chance.

Any words on which 15 or more of you agreed were called me or it words. The theory predicts all 188 words should be me or it words. By chance one out of 20, or about 10 of the words, would be a me or it word. Actually 15 out of 20 of you agreed on 129 of the words. There were only 53 words on which more than five people disagreed with the others.

Today we are going to see if we agree on a different way of judging these words.

First let us consider the it words where the spotlight is on the other person or object that you are interacting with (draws diagram). Now the theory predicts that you will use some words if you are attracted to this person and other words if you are repulsed by this person (points to x in the diagram). So the question you must ask yourself is, "Do I use this word when I want to get closer to or help this person, or do I use this word when I want to get further away from or *change* this person?" Now you must be careful on one point: an attraction word is not necessarily an attrac*tive* word. Consider the word "envious." When you use the word envious there is an attrac*tion* to the object but it is hardly an attractive feeling. "Horrified" is an example of a word we use when there is a repulsion between us and the object. With these it words we are *not* sorting on the basis of attrac*tive*-repul*sive* but on whether or not an attraction exists between you and the object (points to diagram) or a repulsion. Is this clear?

Put a plus sign by those words we use when an attraction exists, a minus sign by those we use when a repulsion exists. Don't forget to imagine an "I feel" before each word. (The subjects judge the it words.)

Now let's consider the me words. When the spotlight is on you it does not make as much sense to ask about how you feel toward the other as it does to ask about the feeling itself. We use some words when the feeling is positive and other words when the feeling is negative. By "positive" I mean that you want to preserve whatever situation you are in. By "negative" I mean that you want to change or get out of whatever situation you are in. I do not want you to pass any social judgments on the feeling. For example, we may use the word "smug" when the situation is positive. We may use the word "shy" when the situation is negative and we'd like to alter it. We are not considering whether you'd rather see someone else, and maybe even yourself, be shy than smug. Note that if envious were a me word it would be negative in spite of the fact that an attraction exists. Is this clear to everyone?

Put a plus sign by those words we use when our feelings are positive, and a negative sign by those we use when our feelings are negative. (The subjects judge the me words.)

Now we must consider the 53 words that may be either it or me words as far as the data we have goes. Since we don't know which criteria to apply, I would like you to judge these words both by determining whether there is an attraction or a repulsion between you and the other person or object, and by just looking at the feeling and judging it positive or negative. Write down two words by each emotion name: either "attraction" or "repulsion" and either "positive" or "negative."

Note that if envy were on the list you'd write down "attraction, negative." After you have written down both words, put a check mark beside the word that seems to be the most reasonable judgment—this will give us another chance to decide whether the word is an it or a me word. Are there any questions about this? (The subjects judge these words.)

Summary of Instructions

Names used when talking about *it* and: (1) an *attraction* between us and the other—envious; (2) a *repulsion* between us and the other—horrified.

Names used when talking about *me* and: (1) *positive* feelings—smug; (2) *negative* feelings—shy.

THIRD SESSION: EXTENSION-CONTRACTION CHOICE
(SUBJECT OR OBJECT POSITION ALTERED)

As you might guess, the sort you did last time turned out very well. There were only 17 words out of the 188 that we did not get at least 15 of you agreeing on. Also, of the 53 words that were not clearly me or it words, there were 19 that 15 or more of you agreed were better described by either attraction-repulsion or by positive-negative. These can now be classified indirectly as to their "meness" or "itness."

Now let's go to the third step. If the spotlight is on the other and a repulsion exists (draws diagram), then the theory says either you have to make an extension movement to push away or demolish this object (demonstrates) or you have to make a contraction movement to pull back from this object (demonstrates). The theory therefore postulates that we use some names when we are pushing the object away and other names when we are pulling back from the object. "Disapproval" is a pushing-away word. "Displeased"[2] is a pulling-back word. Now I think you can see that we are talking about a primitive innate response that is part *of* the emotion and not what you have learned to do in response *to* the emotion. You may have learned to push away something that displeases you or to pull back from something you disapprove of. We are not rating the word on that, but rather on the initial response of pulling back that is present in being displeased and the immediate pushing away implied in disapproval. Are there any questions about this?

If the word is a pushing-away word, draw an arrow away from you—up on the page (demonstrates). If the word is a pulling-back word, draw an arrow going toward you—down on the page. (The subjects judge the it-repulsion words.)

Now the spotlight is still on the other person but an attraction exists. The person again has to make either an extension or contraction movement—but in a different way. You may either give to the other person, or you may pull yourself to him (demonstrates). We use some words when we extend, others when we contract. "Accepting" is a word we use when we extend. "Wonder" is a word we use when we contract. Note the difference between accepting and receiving. In accepting the extension movement is predominant (demonstrates); in a way you are giving something, as when you accept somebody into a group. In receiving the contraction movement predominates as you pull it to you. We use the word "wonder" when we are contracted, open and taking something in—trying to pull the two together (demonstrates the open mouth and flexed arms portraying wonder). You can see you have to be careful here. Ask yourself what you are really accomplishing; are you mostly giving something or mostly pulling the two of you together?

Again we'll use the arrow away from you as extending and toward you as pulling. (The subjects judge the it-attraction words.)

---

[2] "Displeased" was in the original list of emotion names but was discarded by two of the three judges who culled the list. In fact, I now feel that it is often used to refer to a me emotion and was thus a poor example to use here.

Now let's consider the me words. With the spotlight on you it is easier to look at how you feel instead of what the object is doing to you. First the positive feelings. We use certain words when the feeling has a touch of activeness to it—other words when the feeling is circling, pulled together and relaxed in you. Consider the word "secure": We use it when we have a feeling that is circling, relaxed in us. We can imagine the feeling pulled together in us (demonstrates). Consider the word "smug": We use it when we have a feeling that is more active, almost bubbling out from us. Is this clear to everyone? Put an R by the words we use when the feeling is relaxed, an A by those we use when the feeling is active. (The subjects judge the me-positive words.)

Now let's consider the me words that represent negative feelings. We use some words when the feeling is a withdrawn, squashed-down feeling, other words when the feeling is an active, stirred-up feeling. For example, "depression" is used when we're squashed down, whereas "anxious" is used when the feeling is active and stirred up. Put an S for squashed and an A for active by each appropriate word. (The subjects judge the me-negative words.)

Now we have a group of words that we know are plus or minus, but that we're not sure of as it or me words. Just as we did last time, rate these words using both criteria. First treat the word as an it word and ask if it involves an extension or contraction, then treat it as a me word and ask if it's active or relaxed-squashed. Finally, put a check mark beside the decision that seems most appropriate. In this way we have another chance to attain me-it agreement.

First do the plus words. Use the arrow direction for the first judgment of giving-pulling; the R or A for relaxed and active. Please reread your summary sheets.

Now do the minus words. Use arrows for pushing away and pulling back, A and S for active and squashed.

We are now left with 17 words that are not clearly plus or minus. There are four possible sets of two ratings to use on each word. You can describe the word as pushing or pulling back, giving or pulling together, relaxed or active-pleasant, squashed or active-stirred up. Select the two best terms and write down the arrows or letters. Put a plus or a minus by each arrow or letter. Then check the most applicable of the two.

In the case of the it emotions, where the person is the subject of the emotion, a negative extension implies that the object is being moved as it is repulsed by the subject, while a positive extension implies that the subject is moving as the person goes out to the object. Conversely, a negative contraction involves the subject moving (away from the object), while a positive contraction involves the object being moved (toward the subject). Hence, in Table 13 the vote for negative-extension and positive-contraction choices is noted under "object moving," and the vote for positive-extension and negative-contraction choices is noted under "subject moving."

On the other hand, in the case of the me emotions where the person is the object of the emotion, a negative, passive feeling indicates that the person has been moved (is the object of negative extension from an implicit other), while a positive, passive feeling indicates that the person has been moved toward (is the object of a positive extension from an implicit other). Conversely, a negative, action feeling indicates that the person is moved away from (is the object of negative contraction from an implicit other), while a positive, active feeling indicates that the person is moved toward the implicit other (is the object of positive contraction). Thus, in Table 13 the vote for negative-passive and positive-active choices is noted under "object moving," and the vote for negative-active and positive-passive choices is noted under "subject moving."

Summary of Instructions

Names used when talking about *it*, a *repulsion*, and: (1) *pushing away*—disapproval; (2) *pulling back*—displeased.

Names used when talking about *it*, an *attraction*, and: (1) *extending*, giving—accepting; (2) *contracting*, pulling together—wonder.

Names used when talking about *me*, a *positive* feeling, and: (1) a circling, relaxed feeling *pulled together* in us—secure; (2) an active feeling *bubbling forth* from us—smug.

Names used when talking about *me*, a *negative* feeling, and: (1) a withdrawn, *squashed-down* feeling—depressed; (2) an active, *stirred-up* feeling—anxious.

FOURTH SESSION: PRESENCE-LIKENESS-MEANING CHOICE
(BELONGING-RECOGNIZING-BEING)

We made out better than I thought we would. Of the 181 words rated, 116 were agreed on, 65 were not. The only place we didn't get excellent agreement was on the it-repulsion words—only 50 percent of them came out with 15 or more of you agreeing.

Today we proceed to the fourth aspect of this theory; this aspect has many exciting implications. Let's consider it words: the spotlight is on the other. You've decided on attraction or repulsion and on contraction or extension movements. Now the question is: Movements over what kind of distance? Physical distance? Not necessarily. The theory indicates three different kinds of distance. Consider these figures:

Which two figures are the closest? It depends on the kind of closeness we are talking about. You can see that one kind of closeness or distance is physical, the other has to do with likeness. Now I'm going to make two triangles closer in both these senses:

But I put a barrier around them so that they are separated and can't communicate. In some third sense the triangle on the right and the circle are closest—there is a third type of distance involving free communication.

Now when, because of the attraction or repulsion force between you and the object, you try to traverse one of these distances, a feeling arises in you. We can vary the physical distance by just moving the figures (demonstrates). We can vary the likeness distance by changing what one of the figures is like. We can vary the communication distance by opening up or closing ourselves off from the object (demonstrates). Now if you are trying to vary the physical distance between you and the object, the feeling will have a primitive pulling or pushing quality to it. If you are trying to vary your likeness or the object's likeness, the feeling will have a more stationary, looking-at-it quality. If you are varying the communication distance, the feeling will have either an opening or a closing quality to it.

We use different names according to which distance we are trying to traverse. If you are trying to get closer physically, you might use the word "fascinated."[3] Note how you can almost feel a physical pull in this word. If you are looking at what the object is like, you might use the word "impressed." Note how there is no physical pull in impressed—just a looking at what the object is like. If you are trying to vary communication distance, you might use the word "wonder"—note the opening quality, which differs from a pulling or a stationary looking. (The subjects judge the it-attraction-contraction words.)

Now we'll do the pulling-back words. We use some words when we are trying to physically get away; "afraid" is such a word—note the pulling element. We use other words when we are standing there looking at what the other's like and we don't like what we see; "horror" is such a word—note the staring quality. We use still other words when we are trying to shut out some ideas that bother us; "apprehension" is such a word—note the tunneling in of what we're thinking about. (The subjects judge the it-repulsion-contraction words.)

Now consider the giving words. We use some words when the giving is *stretched* over physical distance, such as the word "protective"; other words where the giving involves *looking* at what the person is like or has done, such as the word "pity"; other words when we are opening up to the person, such as "accepting." Try to distinguish between the stretch of protection, the looking of pity, and the opening of accepting. (The subjects judge the it-attraction-extension words.)

Now we'll consider the pushing-away words. We can push away physically—"anger"; look at something and try and change what it's like—"scorn"; close something out—"re-

_____
[3] This was probably an unfortunate choice as an example word.

jecting." (The subjects judge the it-repulsion-extension words.)

The me words are always used when you think the other person is doing something to you. If he has just given you something, you will feel a relaxed, positive feeling. Some of the relaxed-positive feeling words are used when you are given something to help your body. Others are used when you are given something that helps how you look at yourself; still others are used when your soul is helped. There are some examples: "contented" is used when your body is at ease; "virtuous" is used when you look at yourself and like what you see; "calm" is used when your soul is at ease. (The subjects judge the me-positive-relaxed words.)

Now suppose the other person is pulling you to get the two of you together. Then you'll have an active positive feeling. If he's pulling you physically the word will reflect the force he's pulling from your body; you may use a word like "confident." If he's pulling on what you're like, you'll use a word like "pride" that refers to you looking at yourself. If he's opening up to you, your soul will be given direction and you'll use a word like "destined." (The subjects judge the me-positive-active words.)

If the other person is pushing you away, you'll feel a negative, squashed feeling. If he's pushed physically, you'll use a word that has bodily references like "depressed." If he's pushed against what you like, how you look at yourself will suffer and you'll use a word like "ashamed." If he's closed your soul out, you'll feel you have no direction and use a word like "worthless." (The subjects judge the me-negative-squashed words.)

Lastly, if the other is pulling back from you physically, your body will feel activated and you may use a word like "anxious." If he's pulling back from what you like, you'll look bad to yourself and use a word like "guilt"; and if he's closed himself off from you, your soul will be stirred up and you may use a word like "preposterous."[4] (The subjects judge the me-negative-active words.)

[4] "Preposterous" was in the original list of emotion names, but was discarded by two of the three judges who culled the list.

Summary of Instructions

Names used when talking about *it*, an *attraction*, a contraction, and: (1) a *pulling*—fascinated; (2) a *looking*—impressed; (3) an *opening*—wonder.

Names used when talking about *it*, a *repulsion*, a contraction, and: (1) a *pulling back*—afraid; (2) a *looking at*—horror; (3) a *closing off*—apprehension.

Names used when talking about *it*, an *attraction*, an extension, and: (1) a *stretching out*—protection; (2) a *looking*—pity; (3) an *opening up to*—acceptance.

Names used when talking about *it*, a *repulsion*, an extension, and: (1) a *pushing away*—anger; (2) a *looking at*—scorn; (3) a *closing out*—rejection.

Names used when talking about *me*, a *positive, pulled-together* feeling, and: (1) the *body* at ease—contented; (2) you *looking* good—virtuous; (3) the *soul* at ease—calm.

Names used when talking about *me*, a *positive, bubbling-forth* feeling, and: (1) the force from *body*—confident; (2) you *looking* good—proud; (3) the *soul* being given direction—destiny.

Names used when talking about *me*, a *negative, squashed-down* feeling, and: (1) the *body* having lost force—depressed; (2) you *looking* bad—ashamed; (3) the *soul* having no direction—worthless.

Names used when talking about *me*, a *negative, stirred-up* feeling, and: (1) the *body* being affected—anxious; (2) you *looking* bad—guilty; (3) the *soul* being stirred up—preposterous.

FIFTH SESSION: INVOLVED-DETACHED CHOICE[5]

Well, we didn't do so well last time; but we did far better than chance. There were 165 words rated, not including the example words. Of these there was agreement on 98 of the words, but no significant agreement on 67 of the words. In order to get a classification of these 67 words, I have simply taken the category that most of you checked.

Today we have 24 different groups of words. It-attrac-

[5] This choice was not described in the text.

tion-extension-presence words, it-attraction-extension-likeness words, and so on. Often the words in these 24 clusters will be almost synonymous. There are, however, subtle differences in the words and the emotions they represent. Today and tomorrow we will check out the last two predictions the theory makes.

After we decide it or me, plus or minus, extension or contraction, and which type of distance we're interested in varying, the theory says we decide whether we may or may not be involved emotionally with the object. Now that may seem funny to say because all the words name emotions and in all you're involved with the object. But the theory says you are not always involved in the same way. Rather than going into detail about the two types of involvement, I will give you an example and I think you'll see what I mean.

We use the word "angry" when we are emotionally involved. We use the word "exasperated" when we are not so involved. Notice that when you're angry you seem bound up with the other person in a more intense way than when you are just exasperated. Do you all see what I mean? I'm not saying you can't get extremely exasperated; I'm saying that it still *feels* different from anger. It's just not as hot no matter how intense it is. All right, I'd like you to sort these two pages in that way. Put an *E* if you're emotionally involved. Put an *N* if you're not so involved.

All the words on these two pages are it words, and you're trying to vary physical distance. Page one has repulsion words; page two has attraction words. The left column has contraction words, the right column has extension words. I'm telling you this so that you will judge the words against other words like them, so that attraction or repulsion will not bias your estimate of involvement. Every time you change a column or page, you must remember that you're dealing with a different kind of word. (The subjects judge the words.)

Now we will consider the it words that you use when you're varying the likeness distance. We have the same distinction but, since these words do not reflect violent physical movements, even the emotionally involved words sound tamer than the more physical words.

An example of a word we use when we're emotionally involved is "contemptuous." A word used when we're not so involved is "disapproval." Can you all see how contemptuous is hotter—how you're more wrapped up and involved in the action than in disapproval? Again there are really four sets of words—the left and right columns on each of the two pages. (The subjects judge the words.)

Now we'll consider the it-communication distance words. These words are even further removed from the physical so your standard of judgment as to what is emotionally involved must change again. "Apprehensive" is an emotionally involved word; "displeased" is a not-so-involved word. The words are arranged as before. (The subjects judge the words.)

When we consider the me words there is no object to be emotionally involved with or not involved with. An analogous division may be made, however, if we ask whether the feeling is deep or shallow. Deep feelings strike at your core or roots—if negative they bother you more, if positive they are more wonderful. If the distance is physical we may use a word like "depressed" if the feeling is deep. We may use a word like "fatigued" when the feeling is shallow. Note how depression penetrates you while fatigue is on the surface.

Again let me remind you that there are four different sets of words on these two pages. Each column has a different kind of word in it. (The subjects judge the words.)

The me words that are looking-at-oneself words may be divided in the same way. An example of a deep word is "guilty"; an example of a surface word is "apologetic." Again the words in each column are similar. (The subjects judge the words.)

The me words that involve one's soul may be divided similarly. If the feeling is deep, we might use the word "worthless"; if the feeling is surface, the word "useless." Can you see the difference? (The subjects judge the words.)

Summary of Instructions

Names used when talking about *it, presence,* and: (1) emotionally *involved*—anger; (2) *not* so involved—exasperated.

Names used when talking about *it, likeness,* and: (1) emotionally *involved*—contemptuous; (2) *not* so involved—disapproval.

Names used when talking about *it, meaning,* and: (1) emotionally *involved*—apprehension; (2) *not* so involved—displeased.

Names used when talking about *me, presence,* and: (1) *deep* feelings—depressed; (2) *surface* feelings—fatigued.

Names used when talking about *me, likeness,* and: (1) *deep* feelings—guilty; (2) *surface* feelings—apologetic.

Names used when talking about *me, meaning,* and: (1) *deep* feelings—worthless; (2) *surface* feelings—useless.

SIXTH SESSION: EXPRESS-INHIBIT CHOICE (FLUID-FIXED)

Well, we only did fairly well last time. A lot of words hit 14 instead of the required 15 agreements. Of the 177 words rated we would expect nine to have 15 or more agreements if only chance operated. Actually there were 99 words that were agreed on. The 78 words that did not meet the required level of agreement were decided on by a simple majority vote.

I have kept the words on the same pages as before, but I've put the emotionally involved words at the top of each column (demonstrates) with a space separating them from the not-so-involved words. Thus, you now really have 48 different groups of words. There are 12 pages and four different groups on each page. Thus, a group of words may be it words, attraction words, pulling-together words, physical-distance words, and emotionally involved words. Is that clear? You should do one group at a time, pausing for breath between each group.

To understand the sixth and last prediction that the theory makes, let us consider the words "angry" and "hate." What is the difference between these words? The theory claims, and most of you agree, that we use angry and hate when we're trying to push the other person away. The theory goes on to say that we use angry when we are *able* to do something about this urge to push him. We use hate when we are *unable* to do anything about this urge to push him. Note how the word angry expresses much more *movement* than the word hate. Hate is frozen anger.

Let me give you another example. "Afraid" is a word that has movement in it; you can run away. "Terror" is a word that is frozen; there is nothing you can do. Is that clear?

Now you must be careful of words where you are trying to vary likeness or communication distance. The very fact that you are not moving in physical distance may seem to make the feeling frozen when it is not. Therefore, judge these words in relation to the other words in their group. Most groups will probably have half movement and half frozen words. Some groups may have as few as one word that is moving or frozen. In any case, judge the word in its own group. (The subjects judge the it-repulsion words.)

The attraction words may be sorted in the same way. Sometimes you can do what you want, sometimes something blocks it. We use the word "thankful" when we are able to give. The word has movement. We use the word "esteem" when we are unable to give. When the person is too far off to give him thanks, you give him esteem. Esteem is a more stationary word. Is this clear? (The subjects judge the it-attraction words.)

Now we will decide on the me words. There is no object to move toward or against, so we can't speak of frozen movement. But we can speak of being able to get rid of the feeling or not. First we'll consider the negative feelings, where you would like to shake off the feeling. We use the word "ashamed" when we can get rid of the feeling fairly easily. We use the word "despair" when it's not easy to get rid of the feeling. That is, there is more you can do about feeling ashamed, so it usually doesn't last as long as despair, which you can't do much about.

Both ashamed and despair are deep rather than shallow feelings. A hard-to-get-rid-of shallow feeling may seem *less* hard to get rid of than an easy-to-get-rid-of deep feeling, so always judge the word against the other words in its group. Is the reason for this clear? (The subjects judge the me-negative words.)

Now consider the positive feelings. You don't want to get rid of these but the same question may be asked: How big a disturbance does it take to make you lose the feeling? If the feeling is one that can be easily lost we may use the word "comfortable." If the feeling is more stable, harder to lose, we may use the word "contented." Think for a second to pick up the difference. Both "comfortable" and "contented" are shallow words. Be sure to judge the word in its group as the deeper feelings are harder to lose. (The subjects judge the me-positive words.)

Summary of Instructions

Names used when talking about *it,* a *repulsion,* and: (1) being able to do something, more *movement* — angry, afraid; (2) being unable to do something, more stationary, *frozen* — hate, terror.

Names used when talking about *it,* an *attraction,* and: (1) *movement* — thankful; (2) more *stationary* — esteem.

Names used when talking about *me,* a *negative* feeling, and: (1) *easy* to get rid of — ashamed; (2) *harder* to get rid of — despair.

Names used when talking about *me,* a *positive* feeling, and: (1) *easy* to lose — comfortable; (2) *harder* to lose — contented.

RESULTS

While the major results have been presented in Chapter Three (see Table 11), some interesting data on individual differences in the ability to use the words may be summarized as follows.

INDIVIDUAL DIFFERENCES

It might be expected that subjects will vary in their ability to use the emotion names accurately. To determine the extent of this variation, individual error scores were calculated for each of the six testing days. (It will be recalled that on each day the names were sorted on the basis of a different choice.) An error score consisted of the number of times a subject disagreed with the majority of the subjects in the usage of a word. However, an error was counted only in those cases where a significant number of subjects had agreed on the word's usage. The means, standard deviations, and split-half reliability coefficients of the error scores for each of the six testing days are shown in Table 12.

TABLE 12
MEANS, STANDARD DEVIATIONS, AND RELIABILITIES
OF ERROR SCORES AND THEIR CORRELATIONS WITH VERBAL APTITUDE

| | Test Day | | | | | |
	1	2	3	4	5	6
Mean	15.6	7.0	14.6	25.5	12.8	17.6
Standard deviation	7.8	4.1	8.8	4.0	5.3	5.5
Reliability coefficient[a]	.80	.80	.89	.23	.53	.45
Correlation with verbal aptitude[b]	−.67	−.61	−.44	−.02	−.65	−.28

[a] Split-half reliabilities corrected by the Spearman-Brown formula.
[b] For 20 subjects a correlation of −.44 is significant at the .05 level.

A person with high verbal aptitude is a person who knows the meanings of many words; that is, there are a great many words that he can use accurately. Since emotion names are words, it might be expected that a person with a high verbal aptitude will know how to use emotion names more accurately than a person with low verbal aptitude. If, however, a person with a high verbal aptitude is asked to use emotion words in ways that had no relation to their ordinary usage, then he should not be able to use the words with any more accuracy than a person with low verbal aptitude. But if he is asked to use emotion words in the way in which they are ordinarily used, he should be able to use the words with more accuracy. Therefore, if emotion names are ordinarily used in accordance with the six choices that have been described, a person with high verbal aptitude should have a low error score. On the other hand, if the ordinary usage of emotion names has no relation to the six choices, a person with high verbal aptitude should have an average or perhaps even a high error score.

The subjects' verbal aptitude scores have a mean of 580 and a standard deviation of 63. The reliability of the verbal aptitude test for a sample with a standard deviation of 63 is .81. The correlations between the error scores and verbal aptitude are also shown in Table 12.

It may be observed that, in fact, there is a considerable negative correlation between verbal aptitude and error score. When the truncated range of scores is considered, the agreement is quite remarkable. The only exception to this pattern occurred on the fourth day of testing when the presence-identity-existence choice was used to divide the emotion words. This would seem to indicate that on the fourth day subjects reached agreement on the basis of some factor other than a factor actually underlying word usage.

Since words reflecting a person-as-subject choice were sorted on the basis of different principles than were words reflecting an other-as-subject choice, separate error scores were calculated for these two sets of words. On the fourth day the error scores for words reflecting a person-as-subject choice correlated $-.30$ with verbal aptitude. On the other hand, the error scores for words reflecting an object choice correlated $+.28$ with verbal aptitude. On the other testing days there was no such discrepancy between the two groups of words. It may be concluded that when a person-as-subject choice has been made, the criteria used to determine whether a presence, identity, or existence choice has been made is adequately stated, but when an object choice has been made the criteria are inadequate.

Appendix C

154 EMOTION NAMES AND DATA ON THEIR USAGE

Table 13 presents the data on the usage of 154 emotion names. In all cases, 20 subjects rated each word on each choice. When numbers did not total to 20 the remaining subjects had used a question mark to indicate uncertainty as to the names' meaning. An asterisk by a number indicates that the number of subjects is significant. The italicizing of a number indicates that the experimenter voted for the alternative in order to break a tie. The abbreviation Ex. indicates the emotion name was used as an example for the choice.

TABLE 13

NUMBER OF SUBJECTS REFERRING EACH EMOTION NAME TO EACH ALTERNATIVE OF THE DIFFERENT CHOICES

Choices

	Person is Subject-Object (It-Me)		Attraction-Repulsion (To-Away)		Subject-Object moving		Presence-Likeness-Meaning (Belonging-Recognition-Being)			Involved-Detached		Express-Inhibit (Fluid-Fixed)	
abhorrence	19*	1	0	20*	7	13	11	7	2	11	9	5	15*
accepting	16*	3	20*	0	Ex.		Ex.			3	17*	20*	0
admiration	20*	0	20*	0	9	11	3	17*	0	9	11	3	17*
affection	20*	0	20*	0	16*	4	15*	4	1	14	6	19*	1
afraid	Ex.		0	20*	19*	1	Ex.			14	6	Ex.	
alarmed	16*	4	0	20*	16*	4	5	12*	3	11	9	20*	0
amazed	17*	3	19*	1	0	20*	5	2	13*	8	12	3	17*
ambitious	1	19*	19*	1	0	20*	12*	4	4	8	12	4	16*
amused	15*	5	19*	1	4	16*	7	10	3	2	18*	17*	3
angry	13	7	1	19*	3	17*	Ex.			Ex.		Ex.	
anguish	9	11	0	19*	14	6	12*	2	6	19*	1	2	18*
annoyed	18*	2	0	20*	5	15*	8	11	1	1	19*	18*	2
anxious	2	18*	1	19*	Ex.		Ex.			4	16*	10	10
apathetic	6	13	1	17*	5	14	0	9	10	4	15*	3	17*

TABLE 13—Continued

Choices

	Person is Subject-Object (It-Me)		Attraction-Repulsion (To-Away)		Subject-Object moving		Presence-Likeness-Meaning (Belonging-Recognition-Being)			Involved-Detached		Express-Inhibit (Fluid-Fixed)	
apprehensive	18*	2	3	17*	14	6	1	13*	6	Ex.		7	13
approval	17*	3	20*	0	20*	0	Ex.			1	19*	17*	3
ashamed	Ex.		0	20*	2	18*		Ex.		20*	0	Ex.	
astonished	16*	4	14	6	4	16*	3	2	15*	13	7	7	13
(an) aversion	18*	2	1	19*	9	10	5	2	12*	11	9	15*	4
awe	18*	2	20*	0	1	19*	3	5	12*	15*	5	2	18*
benevolent	11	9	19*	1	20*	0	14*	6	0	1	19*	13	7
blasé	1	18*	8	11	3	15*	9	2	8	4	14	13	5
bored	6	14	0	20*	5	15*	14*	2	4	1	19*	19*	1
cheerful[b]													
complacent	1	19*	11	9	18*	2	6	1	13*	2	18*	5	15*
confident	0	20*	20*	0	7	13	Ex.			12	8	7	13
contemptuous	Ex.		0	20*	4	16*	4	10	6	Ex.		12	8
contented	3	17*	20*	0	20*	0	Ex.			7	13	Ex.	
courageous	2	18*	20*	0	0	20*	12*	7	1	15*	5	*10*	*10*
(a) craving	16*	4	20*	0	5	15*	20*	0	0	18*	2	*10*	*10*
curious	14	6	19*	1	6	14	15*	1	4	3	17*	16*	4

defeated	9	11	1	19*	3	17*	11	3	5	15*	5	13	7
dejected	3	17*	0	20*	1	19*	14*	3	3	17*	3	11	9
delighted	10	10	20*	0	3	17*	7	12*	1	1	19*	14	6
depressed	4	16*	0	20*		Ex.	Ex.	2	0	Ex.	8	4	16*
desirous	18*	2	20*	0	5	15*	18*	2	12*	12	2	14	6
despair	2	18*	0	20*	6	14	6	1	10	18*	9		Ex.
despondent	3	17*	0	20*	1	19*	9	1	10	11	12	10	10
determined	5	15*	18*	2	1	19*	9	1	6	8	6	2	18*
devoted	18*	2	20*	0	18*	2	13*	20*	0	14	11	9	11
dignified	1	19*	20*	0	16*	4	0	9	3	9	19*	3	17*
disagreeable	4	11	1	19*	20*	0	8	10	10	1	17*	15*	5
disappointed	13	7	3	17*	12	8	0	9	7	3	18*	14	6
disbelief	20*	0	4	16*	10	10	4	14*	3	2	18*	5	15*
discontented	12	8	1	19*	9	11	3	3	5	2	14	15*	5
disgusted	16*	4	0	20*	9	11	12*	5	7	6	17*	14	6
dislike	20*	0	0	20*	10	10	8	6	8	3	13	11	9
dismayed	7	13	1	19*	6	14	6			7		13	7
distracted[b]													
distressed	7	13	0	20*	11	9	12*	2	6	12	8	12	8
doubt	14	6	6	14	12	8	3	8	9	3	17*	9	11
dread	18*	2	0	20*	16*	4	7	9	4	17*	3	4	16
eager	2	18*	19*	1	0	20*	17*	1	2	4	16*	15*	5
ecstatic	5	13*	17*	0	2	17*	6	7	6	13	6	14	5
elated	7	13	20*	0	3	17*	6	11	3	9	11	12	8

Table 13—*Continued*

Choices

	Person is Subject-Object (It-Me)		Attraction-Repulsion (To-Away)		Subject-Object moving		Presence-Likeness-Meaning (Belonging-Recognition-Being)			Involved-Detached		Express-Inhibit (Fluid-Fixed)	
embarrassed	6	14	0	20*	11	9	3	13*	4	10	*10*	12	8
enjoyment	7	13	20*	0	3	17*	7	10	3	3	17*	16*	4
enthusiastic[a]	11	9	20*	0	16*	4	14*	2	4	9	11	*10*	10
envious	20*	0	Ex.		4	16*	8	8	4	20*	0	8	12
exasperated	13	7	2	18*	5	15*	7	7	6	Ex.		4	16*
excited	10	*10*	17	3	0	20*	18*	1	1	5	15*	18*	2
expectant	12	8	20*	0	8	12	8	3	9	1	19*	18*	2
exultant	3	17*	20*	0	0	20*	8	5	7	15*	5	16*	4
fear (see afraid, frightened)													
free	3	17*	20*	0	8	12	2	6	12*	14	6	12	8
friendly	11	9	20*	0	16*	4	6	1	13*	12	8	18*	2
frightened	17*	3	0	20*	17*	3	15*	5	0	12	8	7	12
frolicsome	0	20*	20*	0	0	20*	15*	5	0	0	20*	19*	1
frustrated[b]													
furious	18*	2	4	16*	2	18*	19*	0	1	20*	0	18*	2
gay[b]													
grateful	15*	5	20*	0	16*	4	10	2	8	5	15*	13	7

	1	2	3	4	5	6	7	8	9	10	11	12	13
gratified	10	10	12	8	6	3	11	4	16*	0	20*	15*	5
grief	17*	3	1	19*	10	2	8	14	6	20*	0	11	9
guilty	18*	2		Ex.		Ex.		10	10	20*	0	19*	1
happy[b]													
hate	Ex.	7	1	19*	2	4	14*	17*	3	19*	1	2	18*
helpless	13	1	14	6	12*	3	5	16*	4	20*	0	18*	2
horrified	19*	14	0	20*	16*	Ex.	2	4	16*	Ex.	19*	1	19*
hopeful	6	10	12	8	5	2	2	16*	4	1	7	17*	3
humble	10		8	12		13*		18*	2	13		18*	2
humiliated[b]													
impatient[b]													
inclined	8	12	20*	0	5	3	12*	7	13	1	18*	9	11
indignant	5	15*	7	13	7	8	3	14	6	18*	1	4	16*
inferior	17*	3	8	12	4	15*	1	18*	2	20*	0	11	9
inspired	3	17*	5	15*	5	7	8	19*	1	0	20*	7	13
interested[b]													
irritated	3	17*	9	11	2	13*	5	11	9	19*	1	0	20*
isolated	8	12	9	11	8	5	7	14	6	20*	0	17*	3
jealous	16*	4	1	19*	5	6	9	11	8	3	17*	4	16*
joyful	5	15*	16*	4	3	11	6	20*	0	0	20*	16*	4
liking	6	14	8	12	10	6	4	3	17*	0	20*	0	20*
loathing	17*	3	5	15*	3	5	12	15*	5	19*	1	0	20*
lonely	7	13	12	8	7	6	7	19*	1	20*	0	19*	1
love	3	17*	0	20*	6	1	13*	6	14	0	20*	1	19*

TABLE 13—Continued

	Person is Subject-Object (It-Me)		Attraction-Repulsion (To-Away)		Subject-Object moving		Presence-Likeness-Meaning (Belonging-Recognition-Being)			Involved-Detached		Express-Inhibit (Fluid-Fixed)	
ludicrous	1	13*	1	14*	14	3	2	7	8	2	16*	15*	3
lustful	8	12	8	12	20*	0	16*	3	1	16*	4	14	6
malicious	7	13	2	18*	20*	0	11	6	3	13	7	15*	5
meek	1	19*	1	19*	0	20*	8	10	2	6	14	5	15*
melancholy	2	18*	2	18*	1	19*	12*	4	4	12	8	15*	5
modest	3	17*	12	8	20*	0	1	16*	2	10	10	7	13
moral	1	19*	18*	2	17*	3	1	12*	6	19*	1	5	15*
mortified	16*	4	1	19*	16*	4	3	11	6	17*	3	3	17*
nauseated	18*	2	0	20*	12	8	9	3	8	10	10	16*	4
nervous[b]													
nostalgic	11	9	17*	3	3	17*	7	10	3	13	7	1	19*
oppressed	15*	4	1	19*	12	8	12*	1	7	3	17*	4	16*
pain[a]	11	9	1	19*	12	8	19*	0	1	5	15*	10	10
panicked[b]													
passion[b]													
patient	9	11	19*	1	18*	2	5	9	5	8	12*	18*	2
pensive[b]													
perplexed	15*	5	13	7	5	15*	3	4	13*	12	8	7	13
pity	19*	1	17*	3	18*	2	3	4	Ex.	17*	3	7	13

	C1	C2	C3	C4	C5	C6	C7	C8	C9	C10	C11	C12	C13
pleased	2	18*	18*	2	3	16*	1	7	13	0	20*	Ex.	17*
powerful	14	6	7	13	2	5	13*	20*	0	0	20*	3	16*
pride	16*	4	3	17*		Ex.	Ex.	11	9	0	20*	4	5
protective	3	17*	15*	5	0	0	20*	6	14	1	19*	15*	2
rage	6	14	2	18*	3	11	5	18*	2	17*	3	18*	8
rapture	4	16*	2	18*	4	13*	3	16*	3	0	18*	11	9
regretful[a]	3	17*	6	14	5	0	14*	10	10	13	7	11	13
relief	3	17*	9	11	6	8	6	3	17*	1	19*	7	5
remorse	13	7	4	16*	10	8	2	13	7	7	13	15*	14
repentance	4	16*	2	18*	6	10	4	9	11	11	9	6	1
resentful	14	6	3	17*	7	6	10	13	6	18*	2	19*	9
resigned[a]	18*	2	11	9	7	7	0	1	19*	11	9	11	0
respect	18*	2	17*	3	0	13*	18*	6	12	0	20*	20*	12
restrained	10	10	15*	5	5	2	1	9	11	17*	3	8	1
reverence	17*	3	7	13	3	14*	7	5	15*	0	20*	19*	15*
sad	6	14	13	7	3	10	16*	16*	4	20*	0	5	11
satisfied	10	10	16*	4	17*	1	2	2	18*	0	20*	9	1
scornful	7	13	8	12		Ex.		16*	4	20*	0	19*	18*
serene	11	9	9	11	9	1	1	1	19*	0	19*	1	
shame (see ashamed)													
skeptical	10	10	18*	2	8	11	0	10	10	17*	3	19*	1
sorrowful	15*	5	14	6		11	1	7	13	10	10	12	7
startled[b]													
strange	10	10	16*	4	11	6	3	6	14	20*	0	5	15*
successful	15*	5	12	8	2	14*	4	7	13	0	20*	2	18*

TABLE 13 — *Continued*

	Choices												
	Person is Subject-Object (It-Me)		Attraction-Repulsion (To-Away)		Subject-Object moving		Presence-Likeness-Meaning (Belonging-Recognition-Being)			Involved-Detached		Express-Inhibit (Fluid-Fixed)	
superior	9	11	19*	1	6	14	9	10	1	11	9	3	17*
surprised	16*	4	15*	5	3	17*	0	1	19*	3	17*	17*	3
suspicious	18*	2	6	14	15*	5	2	8	10	16*	4	12	8
sympathetic	15*	5	20*	0	17*	3	5	12*	3	*10*	*10*	*10*	*10*
tender	8	12	19*	1	15*	5	2	10	8	15*	5	17*	3
terror	18*	2	0	20*	4	16*	8	12*	0	18*	2	Ex.	
thankful	15*	5	20*	0	16*	4	9	6	5	6	14		
timid	6	14	0	20*	16*	4	4	15*	1	7	13	9	11
triumphant	7	13	20*	0	6	14	7	12*	1	*10*	*10*	16*	4
vain	2	18*	6	14	3	17*	1	14*	5	5	15*	12	8
vexed	16*	4	6	14	12	8	5	13*	2	11	9	7	13
virtuous	1	19*	20*	0	11	9	Ex.			17*	3	8	12
weak	1	19*	0	20*	14	6	18*	1	1	4	16*	4	16*
willful	4	15*	18*	1	4	16*	4	1	15*	6	14	6	14
wonder	20*	0	20*	0	Ex.		Ex.			14	6	4	16*
worried	13	7	8	12	12	8	1	7	12*	19*	1	8	12

a The meaning of the vote on the subject-object moving choice is unclear because of possible error in the it – me placement.
b Data not available.

REFERENCES

Ames, A., Jr. (1951), Visual Perception and the Rotating Trapezoidal Window. *Psychol. Monogr.*, 65(7).

Angyal, A. (1941), *Foundations for a Science of Personality*. Cambridge, Mass: Harvard University Press.

Arnheim, R. (1949), The Gestalt Theory of Expression. In: *Documents of Gestalt Psychology*, ed. M. Henle. Berkeley: University of California Press, 1961, pp. 301-323.

———— (1958), Emotion and Feeling in Psychology and Art. In: *Documents of Gestalt Psychology*, ed. M. Henle. Berkeley: University of California Press, 1961, pp. 334-352.

Arnold, M. B. (1960), *Emotion and Personality. Vol. 1. Psychological Aspects*. New York: Columbia University Press.

Asch, S. E. (1951), Effects of Group Pressure upon the Modification and Distortion of Judgments. In: *Basic Studies in Social Psychology*, ed. H. M. Proshansky & B. Seidenberg. New York: Holt, Rinehart & Winston, 1965, pp. 393-401.

Ax, A. F. (1953), The Psychological Differentiation between Fear and Anger in Humans. *Psychosom. Med.*, 15:433-442.

Balint, M. (1952), *Primary Love and Psychoanalytic Technique*. New York: Liveright, 1965.

Beck, A. T. (1967), *Depression*. Philadelphia: University of Pennsylvania Press, 1972.

———— (1976), *Cognitive Therapy and the Emotional Disorders*. New York: International Universities Press.

Bowlby, J. (1969), *Attachment and Loss. Vol. 1. Attachment*. New York: Basic Books.

Brady, J. V. (1958), The Paleocortex and Behavioral Motivation. In: *Biological and Biochemical Bases of Behavior*, ed. H. F. Harlow & C. N. Woolsey. Madison: University of Wisconsin Press.

Brenner, C. (1974), On the Nature and Development of Affects: A Unified Theory. *Psychoanal. Quart.*, 43:532-556.

Briggs, J. L. (1970), *Never in Anger*. Cambridge, Mass.: Harvard University Press.

Bull, N. (1951), The Attitude Theory of Emotion. *Nerv. Ment. Dis. Monogr.*, No. 81.

Buytendijk, F. J. J. (1950), The Phenomenological Approach to the Problem of Feelings and Emotions. In: *Feelings and Emotions; the Mooseheart Symposium*, ed. M. L. Reymert. New York: McGraw-Hill, pp. 127-141.

Calkins, M. W. (1910), *A First Book in Psychology*. New York: Macmillan.

Cannon, W. B. (1915), *Bodily Changes in Pain, Hunger, Fear and Rage*. New York: Appleton.

165

——— (1927), The James-Lange Theory of Emotions: A Critical Examination and an Alternative Theory. *Amer. J. Psychol.*, 30:106-124.

Chein, I. (1972), *The Science of Behavior and the Image of Man.* New York: Basic Books.

D'Arcy, M. C. (1947), *The Mind and Heart of Love, Lion and Unicorn.* Cleveland, Ohio: World, 1956.

Davitz, J. R. (1969), *The Language of Emotion.* New York: Academic Press.

Dembo, T. (1976), The Dynamics of Anger. In: *Field Theory as Human-Science,* ed. J. de Rivera. New York: Gardner Press, pp. 324-422.

Deming, B. (1971), On Anger. In: *We Cannot Live without Our Lives.* New York: Viking Press, 1974, pp. 36-51.

de Rivera, J. (1961), A Decision Theory of the Emotions. Unpublished Doctoral Dissertation, Stanford University, Stanford, Cal.

——— (1968), *The Psychological Dimension of Foreign Policy.* Columbus, Ohio: Merrill.

——— (1976), *Field Theory as Human-Science.* New York: Gardner Press.

Dewey, J. (1895), The Theory of Emotion. II. *Psychol. Rev.*, 2:13-32.

Doi, T. (1973), *The Anatomy of Dependence,* trans. J. Bester. Tokyo, New York, San Francisco: Kodansha.

Ekman, P., Sorenson, E. R., & Friesen, W. V. (1969), Pan-cultural Elements in Facial Displays of Emotion. *Science,* 164:86-88.

Ellerbusch, M. (1976), In One Blinding Moment. *Guideposts,* Sept., pp. 27-30.

Fingarette, H. (1967), *On Responsibility.* New York: Basic Books.

Fromm, E. (1956), *The Art of Loving.* New York: Harper & Row.

Funk, J. (1974), A Phenomenological Investigation of Laughter. Unpublished Masters Thesis, Clark University, Worcester, Mass.

Goffman, E. (1959), *The Presentation of Self in Everyday Life.* Garden City, N. Y.: Doubleday.

Goldstein, K. (1951), On Emotions: Considerations from the Organismic Point of View. *J. Psychol.*, 31:37-49.

Goodman, S. E. (1975), A Clinically-Oriented Phenomenological Investigation of the Experiential Referent of the Word "Anxiety" as Distinguished First from the Experiential Referent of the Word "Panic" and then from the Experiential Referents of the Words "Apprehension," "Fear," and "Terror." Unpublished Doctoral Dissertation, New York University, New York, N.Y.

Green, H. (1964), *I Never Promised You a Rose Garden.* New York: Holt, Rinehart & Winston.

Hastorf, A. H. (1950), The Influence of Suggestion on the Relationship between Stimulus Size and Perceived Distance. *J. Psychol.*, 29:195-217.

Hebb, D. O. (1946), On the Nature of Fear. *Psychol. Rev.*, 53:259-276.

——— & Thompson, W. R. (1954), The Social Significance of Animal Studies. In: *Handbook of Social Psychology,* Vol. 1, ed. G. Lindzey. Cambridge, Mass.: Addison-Wesley, pp. 532-561.

Heider, F. (1958), *The Psychology of Interpersonal Relations.* New York: Wiley.

Hillman, J. (1961), *Emotion.* Evanston, Ill.: Northwestern University Press.

Holt, J. (1964), *How Children Fail.* New York: Dell, 1965.

Izard, C. E. (1971), *The Face of Emotion.* New York: Appleton-Century-Crofts.

Jager, B. (1971), Horizontality and Verticality: A Phenomenological Explanation. In: *Duquesne Studies in Phenomenological Psychology,* Vol. I, ed. A. Giorgi, W. F. Fischer, & R. VonEckartsberg. New York: Humanities Press, 1973, pp. 212-235.

REFERENCES 167

James, W. (1890), *The Principles of Psychology*. New York: Dover, 1950.
———— (1902), *The Varieties of Religious Experience*. New York: Longmans, Green.
Johnson, W. B. (1938), Euphoric and Depressed Moods in Normal Subjects. Part II. *Character & Pers.*, 6:188-202.
Kane, R. (1976), Two Studies on the Experience of Depression. Unpublished Masters Thesis, Clark University, Worcester, Mass.
Kelly, G. A. (1965), The Threat of Aggresion. *J. Hum. Psychol.*, 5:195-201.
Koffka, K. (1935), *Principles of Gestalt Psychology*. New York: Harcourt, Brace, & World.
Kreilkamp, T. (1970), The Dimensions of Psychological Distance. Unpublished Doctoral Dissertation, New York University, New York, N. Y.
Laird, J. D. (1974), Self-attribution of Emotion: The Effects of Expressive Behavior on the Quality of Emotional Experience. *J. Pers. Soc. Psychol.*, 29:475-486.
Lau, J. (1974), A Phenomenological Investigation of a Group of Positive Emotions. Unpublished Masters Thesis, Clark University, Worcester, Mass.
Lazarus, R. S. (1968), Emotions and Adaptation: Conceptual and Empirical Relations. In: *Nebraska Symposium on Motivation*, ed. W. Arnold. Lincoln: University of Nebraska Press.
Lerner, M. T. (1974), Social Psychology of Justice and Interpersonal Attraction. In: *Foundations of Interpersonal Attraction*, ed. T. Huston. New York: Academic Press, pp. 331-351.
Lewin, K. (1935) *Dynamic Theory of Personality*. New York: McGraw-Hill.
Lindsay, J. (1975), A Phenomenological Investigation of Elation, Gladness, and Joy. Unpublished Masters Thesis, Clark University, Worcester, Mass.
Lorenz, K. (1952), *King Solomon's Ring*, trans. M. K. Wilson. New York: Crowell.
Lundholm, H. (1921), The Affective Tone of Lines. *Psychol. Rev.*, 28:43-60.
Lynd, H. M. (1958), *On Shame and the Search for Identity*. New York: Harcourt, Brace.
MacArthur, D. (1964), *Reminiscences*. New York: McGraw-Hill.
Marcel, G. (1967), Desire and Hope. In: *Readings in Existential Phenomenology*, ed. N. Lawrence & D. O'Connor. Englewood Cliffs, N. J.: Prentice-Hall, pp. 277-285.
Marston, W. M. (1928), *Emotions of Normal People*. New York: Harcourt, Brace.
May, M. A. (1948), Experimentally Acquired Drives. *J. Exp. Psychol.*, 38:66-77.
McDougall, W. (1908), *An Introduction to Social Psychology* (3rd edition). Boston: Luce, 1910.
Mead, G. H. (1934), *Mind, Self and Society: From the Standpoint of a Social Behaviorist*, ed. C. W. Morris. Chicago: University of Chicago Press.
Mercier, C. (1888), *The Nervous System and the Mind*. New York: Macmillan.
Miller, N. E. (1951), Learnable Drives and Rewards. In: *Handbook of Experimental Psychology*, ed. S. S. Stevens. New York: Wiley, pp. 435-472.
Modell, A. H. (1968), *Object Love and Reality*. New York: International Universities Press.
Mowrer, O. H. (1960), *Learning Theory and Behavior*. New York: Wiley.
Mucchielli, R. (1966), *Introduction to Structural Psychology*, trans. C. L. Markmann. New York: Avon, 1970.
Nahlowsky, J. W. (1862), *Das Gefühlsleben in seinen wesentlichsten Erscheinungen und Beziehungen*. Leipsig: Verlag von Veit, 1907.
Ortega y Gassett, J. (1957), *On Love*. Cleveland, Ohio: World.

168 JOSEPH DE RIVERA

Osgood, C. E., May, W. H., & Miron, M. S. (1975), *Cross Cultural Universals of Affective Meaning.* Urbana, Ill.: University of Illinois Press.
_____, Suci, G. J., & Tannenbaum, P. H. (1957), *The Measurement of Meaning.* Urbana, Ill.: University of Illinois Press.
Paulhan, F. (1884), *The Laws of Feeling,* trans. C. K. Ogden. New York: Harcourt, Brace, 1930.
Piaget, J. (1970), *Structuralism,* trans. C. Maschler. New York: Harper & Row Torchbooks, 1971.
_____ (1971), *Biology and Knowledge,* trans. B. Walsh. Chicago: University of Chicago Press.
Plutchik, R. (1962), *The Emotions: Facts, Theories and a New Model.* New York: Random House.
Pribram, K. H., & Melges, F. T. (1969), Psychophysiological Basis of Emotion. In: *Handbook of Clinical Neurology,* ed. P. J. Vinken & G. W. Brunyn. Amsterdam: North-Holland, pp. 316-342.
Rapaport, D. (1942), *Emotions and Memory.* Baltimore: Williams & Wilkins.
Read, K. E. (1965), *The High Valley.* New York: Scribner.
Ricoeur, P. (1966), *Freedom and Nature: The Voluntary and the Involuntary.* Evanston, Ill.: Northwestern University Press.
Rogers, C. R. (1961), *On Becoming a Person.* Boston: Houghton Mifflin.
Ruckmick, C. A. (1936), *The Psychology of Feeling and Emotion.* New York: McGraw-Hill.
Russell, B. (1967), *The Autobiography of Bertrand Russell.* London: Allen & Unwiss.
Russell, F. (1904-1905), *The Pima Indians. U. S. Bureau of Amer. Ethol. Ann. Rep.,* 26:3-389.
Sartre, J-P. (1948), *The Emotions: Outline of a Theory.* New York: Philosophical Library.
Schacter, S., & Singer, J. (1962), Cognitive, Social and Physiological Determinants of Emotional State. *Psychol. Rev.,* 69:379-399.
Schafer, R. (1964), The Clinical Analysis of Affects. *J. Amer. Psychoanal. Assn.,* 12:275-299.
Seton, P. H. (1965), Uses of Affect Observed in a Histrionic Patient. *Internat. J. Psycho-Anal.,* 46:226-236.
Shand, A. F. (1914), *The Foundations of Character.* London: Macmillan.
Spinoza, B. (1675), The Ethics. In: *The Chief Works of Benedict de Spinoza,* Vol. 2, trans. R. H. Elwes. New York: Dover, 1951, pp. 1-271.
Strasser, S. (1970), Feeling as Basis of Knowing and Recognizing the Other as an Ego. In: *Feelings and Emotions,* ed. M. Arnold. New York: Academic Press, pp. 291-307.
Sullivan, H. S. (1953), *The Interpersonal Theory of Psychiatry.* New York: Norton.
_____ (1956), *Clinical Studies in Psychiatry.* New York: Norton.
Tolman, E. C. (1923), A Behavioristic Account of the Emotions. *Psychol. Rev.* 30:217-227.
Tomkins, S. S. (1962), *Affect Imagery Consciousness. Vol. 1. The Positive Affects.* New York: Springer.
Truman, H. S. (1956), *Memoirs. Vol. I. Years of Trial and Hope, 1946-1952.* Garden City, N. Y.: Doubleday.
Volkan, V. D. (1976), *Primitive Internalized Object Relations.* New York: International Universities Press.

Wapner, S., Werner, H., & Krus, D. M. (1957), The Effect of Success and Failure on Space Localization. *J. Pers.*, 25:752-756.

Werner, H. (1940), *Comparative Psychology of Mental Development*. New York: Harper.

Whitehead, A. N. (1938), *Modes of Thought*. New York: Macmillan.

Whorf, B. L. (1956), *Language, Thought, and Reality*, ed. J. B. Carroll & J. B. Carroll. Cambridge, Mass.: MIT Press.

Wolff, K. H. (1964), On "Surrender." In: *Interpersonal Dynamics*, ed. W. G. Bennis et al. Homewood, Ill.: Dorsey, pp. 44-52.

Wundt, W. (1897), *Outlines of Psychology* (3rd revised edition). New York: Strechert, 1907.

INDEX

171

174

Perception, 71-72, 74, 86, 95, 100, 121;
  see also Physiognomic perception
Personality; see Individual differences
Phenomenology, 5, 78
Physiognomic perception, 21, 29
Physiological effects, 19, 86-87, 133
Piaget, J., 36, 43, 168
Pity, 106, 111
Plato, 24
Pleasure-unpleasure, 7, 16-17, 26, 103
  as basis of emotion, 19
Plutchik, R., 2-3, 15, 105, 168
Position
  alternation of, 40-43, 69, 73, 141-144
  defense of, 88, 93
  loss of, 85
Postural attitude, 18, 21, 33, 49
Power, 86, 89
Pribram, K. H., 30-31, 34, 100, 168
Pride, 56, 61-62
Primary-process thought, 27, 28
Primitive attitude, 27, 30
Projects; see Concerns of person

Rage, 81
Rapaport, D., 21-23, 27, 31, 32, 34, 35,
  104, 168
Read, K. E., 125, 127-128, 168
Reality, 86, 96, 124
  assertion of, 46, 79, 82-84
  of concepts, 3-4, 76-77
  distortion of, 81, 90
  paradox in, 87
  of self, 64
  social, 30, 88-89, 97, 103
Recognition, 53-62, 65, 68
Reinforcers, 42
Rejection, 64, 66, 67, 83
Relief, 132
Respect, 90, 111
Response, emotional, 95, 130-132
Responsibility, 78-80, 82, 83, 85, 90,
  93, 94, 112
Ricoeur, P., 94, 168
Rights, 80, 92
Risk, 93
Ritual, 128
Rogers, C. R., 63, 168
Ruckmick, C. A., 105, 168

Russell, B., 123, 168
Russell, F., 87, 168

Sartre, J. P., 27-31, 34, 100-102, 168
Schacter, S., 19, 21, 168
"Schadenfreude," 125-126
Schafer, R., 4, 6, 8, 22-23, 76, 168
Schlosberg, H., 4, 8
Security, 45-51, 71
Self
  boundary dissolution, 29-30, 34, 122
  capacity to have, 129
  ideal, 53-55, 64
  -image, 88
  material, 52-53, 65
  as object of emotion, 44-45, 85, 112
  -possession, 124
  real, 64
  -reliance, 126
  -responsibility, 82, 85
  social, 53-54, 65
  spiritual, 65
  unconscious, 32, 34
Semantic differential, 125
Separation, 49, 82, 83, 86, 127, 129
Serenity, 64, 66
Seton, P. H., 23, 168
Shame, 6, 56, 60-62
Shand, A. V., 105, 168
Shyness, 57-58
Singer, J., 19, 21, 168
Skeletal system, 18, 86
Skinner, B. F., 42
Sorenson, E. R., 20, 166
Sorrow, 64-66
Space, psychological, 37, 65-68, 73, 83,
  121-122
  dimensions of, 67-70, 121-122
Spinoza, B., 86, 105, 168
Stengel, B., 5, 8
Stimulus-response theory, 15, 130-132
Strasser, S., 129, 168
Structural analysis, 77, 84
Structural change, 82
Structural theory of emotions, 35-37,
  77, 86, 95-104
  tests of, 99, 116-119, 120-122, 129
Structure
  of body affects, 87

ABOUT THE AUTHORS

HARTVIG DAHL received his M.D. from the University of Illinois in 1946. He completed his psychiatric residency at the Mennninger School of Psychiatry in 1952 and graduated from the San Francisco Institute of Psychoanalysis in 1960 while practicing psychoanalysis in Seattle. He studied experimental psychology at New York University under a Special Research Training Fellowship from N.I.M.H. (1964-1967) and held an N.I.M.H. Research Scientist Development Award at the Research Center for Mental Health at New York University (1967-1972). Since 1972 he has been on the faculty of the Program for Research Training in Psychiatry at the Downstate Medical Center of SUNY. He is also codirector of research of the New York Psychoanalytic Institute.

JOSEPH DE RIVERA began his study of the emotions in 1953 when, as a senior at Yale, he investigated the physiological differences between fear and anxiety. On entering the Medical Service Corps, he began studying the effects of anxiety and happiness in flight trainees. This work evolved into his Ph.D. dissertation on emotions at Stanford University in 1961. When he began to teach at Dartmouth College, he became involved in social psychology and the emotional processes involved in the making of foreign policy decisions, an interest which lead to the publication of *The Psychological Dimension of Foreign Policy* in 1968, while he was on the graduate faculty at New York University. In 1970 he began teaching at Clark University and developing a phenomenological (rather than biological) perspective to the study of emotions and motivation. This new perspective led to the reinterpretation of field theory presented in *Field Theory as Human-Science* (1976) and the view of emotions presented in this monograph. Dr. de Rivera is currently Director of the Social Psychology Program at Clark University.

PSYCHOLOGICAL ISSUES